"Every successful business hits a wall at some point. This book's candid insights and real-world examples are a masterclass in navigating the inevitable complexities of facing bottlenecks, cultural challenges, or leadership team obstacles. Crosby and Cleveland provide the tools and inspiration not only to survive but thrive in a high-growth environment. This book is essential reading for any leader striving to break through to the next level."

Sam Graham, CEO, Diversified Trust Company

"In the fast-paced world of high-growth leadership, every organization faces inevitable obstacles. But with the right framework, these challenges can be transformed into opportunities. *Running the Gauntlet* provides exactly that—a roadmap for leaders to navigate the complexities of scaling, ensuring alignment, and maintaining organizational health at every stage of growth. Meg and Howard offer invaluable insights that not only help businesses survive, but thrive. This is essential reading for any leader committed to breaking through barriers and achieving long-term success."

Robert Covington, Founder and
Managing Partner, Braemont Capital

RUNNING
THE
GAUNTLET

PROVEN STRATEGIES FOR
HIGH-GROWTH LEADERS

RUNNING
THE
GAUNTLET

MEG THOMAS CROSBY

HOWARD CLEVELAND

AN INC.
ORIGINAL

This publication is designed to provide accurate and authoritative information in regard to the subject matter covered. It is sold with the understanding that the publisher and author are not engaged in rendering legal, accounting, or other professional services. Nothing herein shall create an attorney-client relationship, and nothing herein shall constitute legal advice or a solicitation to offer legal advice. If legal advice or other expert assistance is required, the services of a competent professional should be sought.

An Inc. Original
New York, New York
www.anincoriginal.com

This work is being published under the *An Inc. Original* imprint by an exclusive arrangement with *Inc. Magazine*. *Inc. Magazine* and the *Inc.* logo are registered trademarks of Mansueto Ventures, LLC. The *An Inc. Original* logo is a wholly owned trademark of Mansueto Ventures, LLC.

Distributed by Greenleaf Book Group

For ordering information or special discounts for bulk purchases, please contact Greenleaf Book Group at PO Box 91869, Austin, TX 78709, 512.891.6100.

Design and composition by Greenleaf Book Group
Cover design by Greenleaf Book Group
Cover image used under license from ©stock.adobe.com/liuzishan

Publisher's Cataloging-in-Publication data is available.

Print ISBN: 978-1-63909-056-3

eBook ISBN: 978-1-63909-057-0

To offset the number of trees consumed in the printing of our books, Greenleaf donates a portion of the proceeds from each printing to the Arbor Day Foundation. Greenleaf Book Group has replaced over 50,000 trees since 2007.

Printed in the United States of America on acid-free paper

25 26 27 28 29 30 31 32   10 9 8 7 6 5 4 3 2 1

First Edition

This book is dedicated to all the battle-weary executives, investors, and board members who are navigating the relentless obstacles to building high-growth companies. We see you, and we appreciate the complexity of the task you are undertaking. Our hope is that our framework can save you some time and torture as you move through the Growth Gauntlet.

"What got you here won't get you there."

—Marshall Goldsmith

Contents

Welcome to the Gauntlet

EVERYONE WANTS GROWTH, but no one is quite prepared for it.

A group of investors came to us several years ago and asked for help with one of their portfolio companies. They had invested in the company just over a year earlier, and the CEO was already asking for more money. The investors wanted us to help them clarify what was going on so they could decide what to do next.

It turns out that the CEO had used the initial investment to grow the business rapidly. He hired multiple executives at high salaries and purchased millions of dollars in new equipment. He was recognized in the industry for how quickly he was scaling. The problem was that the growth wasn't successful or sustainable. None of the newly hired members of the executive team stayed longer than six months, and hundreds of thousands of dollars were lost in severance on these short-termers. New equipment sat idle, and new and old employees left.

The CEO wanted growth, but he wasn't prepared for it. There didn't appear to be any strategy involved in hiring the executives or buying the equipment. They were impulse buys made just for the appearance of growth. While he brought in new leaders and new employees, he did not have the infrastructure in place to leverage them to grow. He wasn't ready to distribute any real authority or decision-making ability, and he didn't play well with others who had opinions different from his. He was the primary culture carrier, and his leadership style and demeanor were causing an alarming amount of turnover among the rank-and-file employees.

The CEO's lack of ability to build a team was his downfall—not his innovative model, his business acumen, his product knowledge, or his financial skill. In the end, he was replaced by the investors because he was not an effective organization builder. The challenges of growing an organization were more than he was prepared for, more than he could handle, and more than he could deliver. He did not understand that *people drive results*.

Growing a business is no easy feat. The volume and pace of work can feel like a gauntlet of never-ending challenges, and CEOs are constantly having to assess what's coming at them from the market, competition, customers, and employees. No two high-growth companies are alike, but they all face common challenges and obstacles. We've helped dozens of CEOs, board chairs, investors, and leadership teams overseeing thousands of employees navigate and overcome those challenges. Through this work, we've identified patterns that we have distilled into a framework to help business leaders see the entire growth progression. Our framework consists of six key imperatives for organization building that we have mapped across four distinct stages of growth. We call it the Growth Gauntlet.

In this book, we will take you through the Growth Gauntlet framework, as well as the experiences, lessons, and insights we've gathered from decades of working with high-growth companies. We'll also give you tools and methods to put the framework into practice in your organization.

Our work is guided by an overarching philosophy: The only way to win is through people. The primary function of an executive team is to set the vision and build an organization in which people will work hard to help turn the vision into reality. Without the commitment, focus, and buy-in of your people, surviving the Growth Gauntlet is simply not possible. This book is specifically written for CEOs who recognize their people are their number one asset. It's for leaders who want to harness their people's individual and collective strengths so they may develop a resilient organization, prepared to pivot and adjust in the face of the inevitable challenges of growth.

What's in It for You

This book is intended to be an immediately usable guide for CEOs, founders, board members, and investors. Using the Six Imperatives for high growth as our guide, the Growth Gauntlet framework is designed to give you a clear understanding of what is needed at each of the Four Stages of Growth so you can meet the demands head-on. After reading it, you will have the following:

- A clear understanding of the entire organizational growth journey
- Insight into using the Six Imperatives as levers to move, build, and sustain your organization
- A road map of the milestones and initiatives required at each Stage of Growth and for each Imperative

- A common framework and vocabulary for aligning around a
  clear growth plan with your team

Dr. Bob Waller, a friend and former CEO of Mayo Clinic, gave
us sage advice when he said, "Organizations grow in the direction
of the questions asked." For this reason, we've concluded each of
the Six Imperative chapters with a section called "Leveling Up: The
Strategic Edge," populated with targeted, Stage of Growth–specific
questions for CEOs to ask themselves and their leadership teams
and for board members to ask CEOs. We crafted these questions to
create opportunities for meaningful reflection and dialogue. These
are meant to serve as a starting point to assess where you are and
what's next as the organization grows and matures.

Many of our clients and the companies we seek to help are backed
by private equity (PE) firms. The size, values, investment theses, and
level of oversight of PE firms vary greatly. "Investing in leadership"
has become a boilerplate statement advertised by many PE firms.
Many firms say it, but most lack the depth of knowledge and experience to support leaders in organization building. Though this book
is not targeted solely to investors, the Growth Gauntlet framework
is a valuable tool for them as it introduces more rigor and objective
measurement tools to the people side of company building by using
a framework to assess leadership, people, and culture.

Throughout these pages, we provide strategic context to a business's growth journey through real-world examples. This book is a
practical guide. Our goal is greater than simply providing insight and
creating "aha" moments. We recognize the excitement that comes
with insight often fades in the face of the relentless day-to-day
demands.

In our business, we serve as an implementation partner and guide
for our clients to help them take the necessary steps to reach the next

level. In this book, we share the same model and methodology we use with our clients to build the leadership and organizational habits, mindsets, and competencies necessary for success.

No One Right Path for Growth

There is no one right path for growth, and we don't prescribe turn-by-turn directions in this book. We are not offering a turnkey system to follow daily or a set of mandatory steps you must take to stay on track. Such an approach is impossible given the variations in size, industries, growth stage, revenue, pace, and culture of different organizations. Rather, we provide the key landmarks to ensure you're on the right path. The best route for your company will vary from other organizations, but the Four Stages of the Growth Gauntlet and the Six Imperatives for high growth will not.

Wherever you are on your growth journey, the Growth Gauntlet will give you the framework to discover where your company is today and find a clear path to the next level. Both descriptive and prescriptive, it is for those who are in the trenches with their teams every day. Whether you are a founder entering a Stage of the Growth Gauntlet that requires new innovation, a first-time CEO taking the reins from a beloved founder who must win over the hearts and minds of a loyal (but often dysfunctional) staff, or a private equity–backed CEO attempting to navigate the expectations of your board, you will find an ally in the Growth Gauntlet.

CHAPTER 1

The High-Growth Survival Plan

GROWTH IS HARD. There isn't a CEO on the planet who would argue otherwise. Entrepreneurs start businesses because they have a great idea or an incredible market opportunity they wholeheartedly believe in. That's the easy part. The road to success is littered with great ideas. Ushering an idea from inception to a stable, year-over-year, predictable, double-digit, high-growth company is one of the most exciting and excruciating challenges a leader will face. Building and scaling a sustainable business is the hard part.

When we talk to CEOs who are grappling with this challenging work—who are logging 100-hour weeks, putting out fires, watching the burn rate, and trying to hang on long enough to raise another round of capital or bring in a whale of a customer—we recognize they are in survival mode. Just as they get a handle on the business, everything shifts. A new reality presents itself and requires a different set of skills and experiences to navigate. We've worked with CEOs who are stretched too thin, frustrated, and overwhelmed by constant growing pains like the loss of an alpha client and its life-sustaining revenue, departing mission-critical employees who take their institutional knowledge with them, legislative changes that erase opportunity and funding, competition that wins the time to market race, software that doesn't hold up to the expectations of the client, customer demand that outpaces operational capabilities, and on and on and on . . . The chaos is palpable.

Our objective is to change that. We aim to bring order and predictability to high-growth businesses and the people who run them because we recognize that most CEOs are experts in the products they build and the markets they serve, but they are not necessarily experts in organization building or people development.

PeopleCap Advisors was born from our own entrepreneurial idea: to help organizations navigate the stages of growth and manage the chaos that comes with it. Howard is a recovering labor and employment attorney with extensive executive leadership coaching experience. Meg is a veteran executive of high-growth companies and was an early member of Google's HR team. Together, we partner with CEOs, founders, board members, and investors to identify and implement effective growth strategies for long-term success.

When we first put our minds and experiences together in 2012, the knowledge economy was in full swing. We recognized the increasing importance of "talent." In fact, we realized the use of the word "talent" to describe workers was itself a shift. Prior to its use in corporate settings, the word "talent" was reserved for professional athletes or movie stars. Corporate adoption of the word signaled a major increase in the value companies were placing on their employees. Leaders who understood this shift and demonstrated they valued their people as their greatest asset possessed a clear winning advantage. With that, we found our deeply shared belief: *People drive results.*

We have been in, or consulting for, high-growth companies for 20-plus years. Our focus is organizational growth and people development. Most founders and entrepreneurs start out with an idea for a product or a service. Their expertise is rarely in managing people. But for a company to scale successfully, leaders must master the ability to achieve their goals through other people. As organizations grow, they add more people, and the more people you add to the team, the greater the complexity in achieving those results. It is for this reason we believe your people strategy is as important as your financial strategy, and we help CEOs build for growth with this core tenet as our guide.

The Four Stages of the Growth Gauntlet, or Mushroom World

In college, Meg had an awful summer internship at a commercial bank manually filing car titles by VIN number. When summer was over, she took her earnings and bought a Nintendo game console and a beanbag chair for her dorm room. Back at school for the fall semester, she and her roommates played a lot of Nintendo, primarily *Super Mario Bros.* She played over and over to the degree she began to see patterns emerge: where the magic mushrooms were hiding; how to evade the Goombas, the Koopa Troopas, and the Piranha Plants; when to go for the gold coins and when to avoid them; when to jump; and when to run. To win the game, she had to make it through the challenges of eight different worlds and ultimately rescue Princess Toadstool from Bowser.

After much practice, she learned how to master one world and unlock the next. But the next world was always completely different! All the knowledge and skills she gained on the previous level didn't apply. There was a whole new set of challenges to overcome. Sometimes, when she was stumped, Meg sought the counsel of more experienced players on how to navigate a certain challenge and level up.

Scaling a high-growth business can feel a lot like navigating the world of *Super Mario*. As soon as you've mastered one world, there's another one waiting to be conquered. Leveling up presents a completely new set of challenges and requires new skills, systems, processes, and people. CEOs of high-growth companies should prepare to traverse the Four Stages of the Growth Gauntlet.

Just as people develop and learn through new experiences and challenges, as Meg did with *Super Mario Bros.*, organizations also develop competencies as they grow. Each of the four stages requires new and more mature organizational competencies, skills, leadership traits, and points of focus. The Four Stages of the Growth Gauntlet chart the growing complexity to allow CEOs and leadership executives to prepare for what's coming and plan for it instead of being blindsided.

What Stage of Growth best describes your company?

1. EMERGE

Key Characteristics: Informal, Ad Hoc, Undefined, Reactive
Getting started is messy, but a mess is not always a bad thing! Businesses, generally, are launched when one or two people have an idea. The early founders and their first few employees form a team. The inaugural team is the simplest unit of an organization; it's like a cell that forms around an idea or opportunity. The focus of this

stage is to prove the business model, product, or market opportunity quickly. During this messy, creative time, the company's identity draws largely from the founder's values and vision, which are organic and unscripted.

Emerge stage companies, also commonly referred to as start-ups, frequently pivot in reaction to client requests and customer feedback. Until they land on a formula for success, there's no reason to expend energy codifying. As Reid Hoffman says of this stage, "Blitzscaling is prioritizing speed over efficiency in the face of uncertainty."[1] The company is free to focus on innovation and is generally unencumbered by anything other than a lack of key resources: people, money, and time.

The required organizational competencies in the Emerge stage are creativity and agility.

2. OPERATIONALIZE

Key Characteristics: Defined, Data-Informed, Focused, Proactive
Aha! Now we're getting somewhere. Once the business has proof of concept—or, more to the point, someone is buying what you are selling—it's time to build the mousetrap, the infrastructure needed to support the operation. In many ways, the Operationalize stage is the most important. It's when the company shifts from being purely entrepreneurial and creative to building the foundation for growth. Processes and systems encompass the practical and technical capacity to serve more customers a consistent quality product or service every time. Anyone can make a great burger. But the real trick is to move from customization to standardization and ensure the process is set up to make the same great burger night after night for 100 people or, eventually, a billion!

Companies often describe the shift from Emerge to Operationalize in terms of "productizing" their offering, and rightly so. For example, in the Emerge stage, they develop technology that can do a lot of things. Different customers ask for different iterations, and the company is reactive; they build whatever the paying customer wants, which results in many one-off products. The shift into the Operationalize stage occurs when they have enough data and experience to be proactive and develop only one product to take to market, which means they can stop customizing for individual requests.

The organizational competencies for the Operationalize stage are internally focused on process development and professionalizing operations. Developing processes to support innovation is a vastly different skill set from innovating itself. Companies often hire people with this skill set from outside to complement the entrepreneur/founder who tends to lead with creativity over process. By this stage, the company has likely grown beyond the initial founding team into multiple specialized teams. This added complexity drives the need for more structured people processes and improved intentional communication.

3. THRIVE

Key Characteristics: Accountable, Data-Driven, Predictable
Bring it on! With the internal operational mousetrap securely in place, the company is poised for breakout growth. They can confidently turn on the spigot of growth and focus on external sales. Ideally, the organization won't be overwhelmed by accelerated growth because processes are in place to accommodate increased sales.

One of the biggest limiting factors in scaling for growth is people. Organizations must recognize the immediate need to bring in new talent and get them up to productivity quickly. That recognition alone is a core growth competency, as are the hiring, onboarding, and training processes necessary to facilitate the influx of new staff.

A digital marketing company was staring down a pipeline of nearly unlimited revenue potential. Customers were lining up at the door. But as sales increased, the team buckled under the weight of the demand. The company had failed to build mechanisms for sourcing, hiring, and training talent quickly and effectively. As they saw it, they didn't have time to recruit or train new hires because they were all focused on working with revenue-producing clients. The shortsighted response limited their ability to take on new clients and led to a collapse. It was an expensive oversight. Ultimately, they had to double back and build the mousetrap for talent acquisition, much like in *Super Mario Bros.*, when you use up one of your lives and have to start over at the beginning of that level.

When processes are firmly in place, the company can grow sustainably.

4. EXPLORE AND EXPAND

Key Characteristics: Strategic, Agile, Innovative, Opportunistic

Let's take this show on the road! For many companies, the Explore and Expand stage is the destination. Those who make it through the Gauntlet and arrive here have a firm foundation and proven successes from which to dream big. It's time to parlay the mousetrap into new products, verticals, geographies, and so on. By now, the organization has strong core competencies and a clearly established and recognizable identity to leverage into new business opportunities.

At this stage, scale comes from taking what has been done successfully and applying it to something new. Growth is no longer exclusively organic, and opportunities such as strategic acquisition come into play.

Though getting here means you have largely survived the Growth Gauntlet, there's no time for complacency. The Explore and Expand stage has challenges too. One of those is keeping products or services fresh and relevant to the market. What started as innovative in the Emerge stage has fully matured, and often, what gets lost in the process—literally and figuratively—is the innovation that got the company where it is in the first place.

We're all familiar with the adage "innovate or die." At this stage, it's important to build innovation *and* Innovation back into the infrastructure. Lowercase "i" innovation refers to incremental innovations that come from the front lines of the business such as upgrading technologies or mining customer data to find efficiencies or optimize existing opportunities. Lowercase innovation is fostered through culture. Uppercase "I" Innovation is blue ocean thinking. It's the "big hairy audacious goal." Uppercase Innovation requires intentional investment in talent and resources to focus on new markets, products, services, and technologies. For example, forming a research and development team, product innovation group, or incubator serves to formalize innovation efforts. Companies in the Explore and Expand stage must utilize and encourage both types of innovation.

The Six Imperatives for High Growth

We've had the privilege of working with companies both large and small. Operating a business with only a few employees is like riding a bike compared to operating a multinational corporation with thousands of people, which is more like captaining the space shuttle. The complexity of the latter mission is exponential, and increasing complexity is what sets each Stage of Growth apart from the next. As the organization becomes more complex in its number of people, products, markets, and capital, it must operate differently.

Looking through the lens of the Four Stages of Growth provides critical context for understanding the specific challenges that companies face as they scale from idea to organizational maturity.

Working with CEOs across all four stages, we began to see the same people-related issues occur time and time again. And they were dramatic enough to stall business growth. When we started to catalog those people-related issues, they reliably fell into one of six buckets: strategy, culture, leadership, talent, organizational structure, and communication. We codified these buckets into the Six Imperatives for high growth. All six will remain essential from the Emerge stage all the way through Explore and Expand. Together, they are the key factors that impact an organization's long-term health and viability.

Each of the Six Imperatives will be thoroughly explored in the upcoming chapters, but here's a quick snapshot.

> **As the organization becomes more complex in its number of people, products, markets, and capital, it must operate differently.**

1. SHARPEN FOCUS: CLEAR VISION CREATES A COMMON PURPOSE.

Employees make decisions every day about how to allocate their time and the company's resources. The best way to ensure they make decisions that lead to forward progress is to have a sharp focus that is clearly understood by everyone in the organization.

2. CALIBRATE CULTURE: DON'T LEAVE CULTURE TO CHANCE.

Culture starts with establishing a set of core values that communicate to employees what behaviors will be rewarded and, conversely, what behaviors will not be tolerated. As an organization grows, goals and strategies change, and the culture must evolve to support those changes.

 ## 3. STRENGTHEN LEADERSHIP: LEADERSHIP IS THE FORCE MULTIPLIER.

Leadership begins with a passionate founder and moves to a distributed team as the company grows. Each leader added to the team changes the dynamic. Building a cohesive and aligned leadership team requires intention and effort.

 ## 4. ELEVATE TALENT: AN ORGANIZATION CAN'T OUTPERFORM ITS TALENT.

Growth demands higher organizational performance. High performance requires raising the bar on talent, which means a constant commitment to developing existing talent, attracting the best new talent, and liberating poor performers.

 ## 5. ALIGN STRUCTURES: STRUCTURE FOLLOWS STRATEGY.

Organizational structures—including people and processes—must evolve to align with the business strategy. Aligning structures leads to increased clarity, efficiency, speed, agility, and accountability.

6. AMPLIFY COMMUNICATION: COMMUNICATION IS THE LIFEBLOOD OF ANY ORGANIZATION.

As you grow, it's harder to keep everyone in the loop. Leaders must drive the sharing of knowledge, information, and feedback across the entire organization in every direction.

Using the Six Imperatives, we help our clients diagnose problems and identify solutions. The Six Imperatives allow leaders to see and understand the "people" side of the business in manageable work streams. Instead of being paralyzed by an ominous and encyclopedic list of all the things they "should" be doing, they are able to focus on these six key areas, each of which comes with its own milestones and initiatives to unlock potential and move the business forward in a healthy and sustainable way.

Think of it like this: Let's say your New Year's resolution is to get in shape. That endeavor involves focusing on more than one area of your life. For example, you might resolve to eat healthier, drink more water, lift weights, commit to some form of cardio, sleep eight hours a night, cut back on sugar and cocktails, and so on. The sum of your efforts moves the needle on your health. The same is true for organizations. Each of the Six Imperatives contributes to overall organizational health. As with any quest to live healthier, the work is constant. We deliberately use the imperative format because the work is never finished. These six key areas are constantly evolving, and a leader must be vigilant to make forward progress in each of the six interrelated areas.

Another way to think about the Six Imperatives is as the levers a leader moves to create value in the organization through people.

Each Imperative has proven methods to unlock growth, and each has its own common mistakes to avoid to prevent wasted time and resources. Actively managing each of the Imperatives greatly enhances a CEO's likelihood of mastering each Stage of Growth and leveling up.

The Growth Gauntlet: A Framework to Predict and Overcome Obstacles

Being the CEO of a high-growth organization is a 24/7 job filled with never-ending challenges: decisions to make, problems to solve, capital to raise, and people to hire. We've witnessed so many war stories over the years we began to refer to the high-growth CEO's journey as running the gauntlet. The path forward feels like it's filled with enemy combatants, armed with a variety of medieval torture devices, whose only job is to take the business down. Most days, it's hard to even see the path because you're constantly in reaction mode—navigating obstacles and existential threats, both real and imagined. You're putting out fires, soothing egos, and counting pennies with an eye on the clock. If you're a private equity–backed organization, these pressures are even more complex.

We get it. Running the gauntlet is excruciating work, but it can be exhilarating, too. We've had the benefit of ushering many leaders and their companies through the gauntlet, and from that experience, we designed this model to help CEOs and leadership teams predict, prepare for, and execute the necessary strategic initiatives to survive the ruthless gauntlet of growth, hence the *Growth Gauntlet*.

The Growth Gauntlet is the marriage of the Six Imperatives and the Four Stages of Growth. The framework started as an internal document we created to guide our work with our clients. When we shared a rough draft of the Growth Gauntlet framework with a client CEO and friend of ours to help him visualize what we were saying, he said, "This is what I've needed. I can see exactly where we are and where we need to go. Can I keep this?" At that moment, we realized how valuable the Growth Gauntlet could be to help guide CEOs and leadership teams. Since then, the Growth Gauntlet framework has helped hundreds of CEOs and executive leaders understand that the pains they are experiencing—while overwhelming—are common for their company's Stage of Growth. And better yet, the Growth Gauntlet is able to provide clarity, direction, solutions, and resources to help them move beyond the chaos.

The Growth Gauntlet

	Stages of Growth			
The Six Imperatives	**Emerge** Informal, Ad Hoc, Undefined, Reactive	**Operationalize** Defined, Data-Informed, Focused, Proactive	**Thrive** Accountable, Data-Driven, Predictable	**Explore & Expand** Strategic, Agile, Innovative, Opportunistic
Sharpen Focus	Primary focus is on proving out product, market, or business model.	Product, market, or business model is proven. Stated corporate purpose/vision exists. The focus is mostly on achieving revenue goals. A goal-setting framework is introduced.	Detailed Strategic Plan exists with budgets, forecasts, and data-driven metrics. Focus is on growing market share. Corporate and individual goals in place.	Business is regularly meeting financial targets. With operations running smoothly, the focus shifts from internal operations to exploring external opportunities. Dual innovation occurs.
Calibrate Culture	Culture is organic, emerging, and is largely a reflection of the personality and priorities of the founder(s).	Culture moves beyond the founder. It is defined in the form of core values and used in some decision-making.	Culture is reinforced through processes like hiring, talent development, performance management, and compensation.	Culture is a driver and used as a lens through which to evaluate strategic opportunities. Culture is defended.
Strengthen Leadership	Organization is founder-led. Leaders wear many hats. Roles are not explicitly defined.	CEO is player/coach with heavy operational responsibilities. Leadership team is loose confederation of functional leaders. Key experienced hires are needed to round out team.	Highly competent, cohesive, aligned leadership team is in place. Each leadership team member owns a key strategy or function critical to success. CEO's time increasingly externally focused on growth.	CEO is mostly focused on strategic opportunities. Leadership team has full ownership of day-to-day operations and wears both functional and strategic hats.

The Six Imperatives	Stage 1	Stage 2	Stage 3	Stage 4
Elevate Talent	Talent is convenient, largely hired and managed by founder. Loyalty is valued over accountability. People know who poor performers are, but there is no process or accountability in place to address them.	More experienced and specialized skills are needed. Performance and accountability are increasingly important. Individual contributors are elevated to managers. HR exists and is mostly transactional.	Organization is building core competencies in recruiting, hiring, developing, and liberating talent. Middle managers are consistently trained and accountable for their team's performance. HR adds strategic talent management function.	Strong leadership and talent pipelines exist. Middle managers are key to driving growth, innovation, and engagement. Chief Human Resources Officer (CHRO) is elevated to the leadership team.
Align Structures	Organization is structured as one undefined team largely all reporting to the founder. Manual processes emerge.	Functional structure is defined. Departments emerge. Processes are being formalized, defined, documented.	Structure is aligned with strategy. Repeatable processes are in place driven by systems, tools, and automation.	Structure is agile and evolves with strategy. Processes are mined for efficiencies, continuous improvement.
Amplify Communication	Communication is informal, often direct from founder. Everyone is in-the-know because of the proximity of the small team. Customer communication is direct, tight loop.	Communication becomes more intentional though still largely top down. Employee and customer feedback are solicited episodically.	Communications protocols, channels, and systems emerge. Employee and customer feedback is regularly solicited and valued.	Comprehensive and strategic internal communications function exists for larger and more distributed customer base and workforce. Multi-directional feedback loops provide data that drives change.

Each growth stage is a building block that sets the foundation for the next stage, and each stage presents a fresh set of challenges that require developing new skills and experiences, mastering new organizational competencies, and achieving new milestones. In other words, the Six Imperatives look very different at each Stage of Growth. The cumulative result of the work outlined in the Growth Gauntlet is a strong and sustainable organization, well positioned to weather the chaos of growth.

Building a sustainable organization is a lot like the New Year's resolution of getting in shape: It requires intention, consistency, hard work, and commitment over a long period of time. As with getting fit, you can't skip a stage. You can't go from the couch to running a marathon without training to build strength and endurance. You can't bench-press 250 until you have bench-pressed 50, 150, 200, and so on. In our experience, if you skip a growth stage or fail to address its unique challenges, you're likely to find yourself backtracking later and wasting precious time and resources in the process.

Every high-growth company has its own products, services, and business model. But one thing all companies have in common is people. People come together to form an organization whose purpose is to achieve the vision and strategy of the business. Those people drive results. The challenge for business leaders is to mobilize and energize people to drive *outsized* results. The Growth Gauntlet helps leaders identify and contextualize their people issues, and it gives them the specific actions to take and levers to pull to accelerate growth and to build a sustainable high-growth organization.

The challenge for business leaders is to mobilize and energize people to drive outsized results.

Knowing what to expect—the challenges, focus, necessary skills, and competencies—gives you the control, clarity, and confidence to navigate the roadblocks ahead. And building a strong, sustainable organization helps you to weather the toughest and most unexpected curveballs that inevitably surface at the most inconvenient times.

Over the next several chapters, we will . . .

- Take you through the entire Growth Gauntlet framework from top to bottom
- Define the Six Imperatives in greater detail
- Chart the evolution of the Six Imperatives across the Four Stages of Growth
- Provide practical, immediately usable tools and resources
- Identify initiatives and milestones for each of the Six Imperatives
- Give you tools to strengthen both your leadership as CEO and the effectiveness of your leadership team
- Track the evolution of your role as CEO across the Four Stages of Growth

Getting Started

Before we dive deep into the Growth Gauntlet in the following chapters, we suggest you take a few minutes to visit our website and take the Organizational Growth Assessment. The survey results will provide a snapshot of where your organization is on the growth journey, which will help orient you as you read the book. The survey is free and can be found by visiting https://www.peoplecap.com/growth-gauntlet.

Wherever you are in your growth journey, we'll be your guides to unlock the next level on the road to building a healthy and sustainable high-growth organization. It will be as satisfying as mastering *Super Mario Bros.* in your dorm room and a whole lot more profitable.

CHAPTER 2

Sharpen Focus

"Greatness starts with a clear vision of the future."

—Simon Sinek

WE'VE EXPERIENCED the Imperative to Sharpen Focus firsthand in our own business. When we started PeopleCap, we wanted to help as many companies as possible. Partly because we were quickly building a service offering and partly because we needed revenue, we took on every project that came our way and said yes to everyone. We changed and customized our services based on each company's desires and needs, and we often revised our marketing materials to fit whatever it seemed like people wanted most. We recently found one of our first proposals and were amused to see the huge range of services we were offering to perform. We were completely reactionary and scattered in our approach.

Once we had several clients under our belt, we paused to get clear about our "Why" and what was most important to us. What were we uniquely qualified to offer? Who were we best equipped to serve? What were our core values? How did we want to serve? What was our vision for the future—both for ourselves and for our clients? Once we got focused, we were able to discern what opportunities to pursue and how to best allocate our time and resources. As a result, we increased our effectiveness and our impact.

The more employees you have, the harder it is to keep the company focused. Meg had a boss once who was known for constantly repeating, "Keep the main thing the main thing." This was his way of saying, "Sharpen Focus." Every day, your employees are making decisions about how they spend their time and your resources. If they are not clear on the company's priorities, you're likely wasting productivity and capital. Clear direction empowers managers and employees to make better decisions because they understand where the company is going and how their role impacts its trajectory.

Sharpen Focus is the first and most important of the Six Imperatives because it's about direction: vision, strategy, and goals. Generally, the Imperatives are equally weighted and represent the pillars necessary to support a solid foundation for successful and sustainable growth. Sharpen Focus is the exception because culture, leadership, talent, structure, and communication must align with a sharp focus.

While this is the most important imperative, it's also the hardest in many ways. Many founder CEOs are creative visionaries whose minds are in a constant state of inspiration. To complicate things, rapid success typically translates to an influx of opportunities knocking on the door. It's easy to get distracted by the flurry of interest and excitement and lose sight of the company's core purpose. Likewise, when times are tough and business is sluggish, there's a temptation to throw everything at the wall to see what sticks. Operational challenges keep us mired in the day-to-day work, prohibiting us from thinking strategically and staying focused on the vision. If you're not grounded in a strong vision backed by strategic initiatives that support the company's goals, losing focus will have you wandering lost in the desert.

Vision = the Why

Vision is the long-term purpose of the company, the North Star, the huge, daunting challenge, the ultimate stretch goal. It's a point on the faraway horizon toward which everyone in the organization sets their course. Your vision becomes the standard against which corporate strategies and goals are set, key decisions are made, and work is aligned.

How does your company complete the following sentence?

"We exist to_____."

The blank space represents the emotional *why* that connects employees to the work they do every day. It should do the following:

- Paint a vivid picture of what your company will achieve
- Be clear, compelling, and unifying
- Invoke passion and commitment
- Excite and energize the entire organization

Increasingly, employees want to be connected to something bigger than a paycheck. The best employees aren't content just going through the motions. People want their work to have meaning, and they expect their company to stand for something. The vision must connect with them in a way that allows them to say, "The work I do is something I want to be remembered for." Employees who are emotionally attached to the company's vision are more invested and they stay longer. They tend to be more engaged, are more willing to accept imperfections, and are more emotionally connected to their work.

It's not uncommon for a leadership team in the Emerge stage to tell us their vision is "to increase shareholder value" or to hit certain revenue targets. Sure, businesses exist to make a profit, but "to increase shareholder value" is not a vision that connects emotionally with employees (particularly if they themselves are not shareholders). In fact, a vision based solely on financial results can be detrimental. Employees will quickly start to resent their work if they feel they are only working to make the executives more money. Or, worse, the company will attract employees whose only loyalty is to their paycheck.

Employees who are emotionally attached to the company's vision are more invested and they stay longer.

A strong vision galvanizes employees. Consider the following powerful vision statements from some of the most successful companies in the world:[2]

"Organize the world's information and make it universally accessible and useful."

—Google

"Bring inspiration and innovation to every athlete in the world."

—Nike

"To be Earth's most customer-centric company."

—Amazon

"To make the best products on earth and to leave the world better than we found it."

—Apple

These statements allow employees to see how their individual roles advance the business pursuit. They articulate what the company values, as well as its direction.

- Google values the accessibility of information.
- Nike wants to do more than sell shoes; they want to inspire athletes.
- Amazon values customers.
- Apple values user experience.

We all know how coveted employment is at these top four global organizations. People want to work for companies that allow them to connect to a larger vision. It's not about simply punching in and punching out. And if that's how your employees view their jobs—if they're not connected to the company's vision—everyone suffers.

Alignment and Accountability = Sweet Harmony

Having a great vision is important; getting people to align around it is critical. It is the CEO's responsibility to make the connection. According to authors and visionary leadership experts Jim Collins and Jerry Porras, "Building a visionary company is 1% vision and 99% alignment."[3] Alignment occurs when everyone in the company is mobilized around a common set of goals that advance the company's business strategy in support of the vision. On the contrary, misalignment causes friction, such as internal politics, competing priorities, undermining others' efforts, rework, confusion, and frustration, all of which interfere with executing on strategy.

One of the first things we do when engaging with a new client is test for organizational alignment. We sit down with each member of the leadership team individually and ask about the business strategy and top priorities for the company. In a well-aligned company, each leader is singing from the same hymnbook in harmony; they are easily able to recite the strategy and key priorities. In a misaligned company, each leader answers differently, singing their own tune and creating a chorus of competing melodies.

We heard this racket from the leadership team at a healthcare company recently. When we asked each leader what the core vision of the company was, no two answers were the same. Some said they were a healthcare company, others said they provided software-enabled marketing, and still others said they were a service provider. The misaligned responses revealed how differently each person approached the allocation of resources and decision-making. CEOs and board members need to stay in tune with the songs their departments are singing and ensure they are aligned, or the whole choir will be out of whack, and the noise will be deafening.

CASE IN POINT: THE DISCONNECTED DEPARTMENT

We witnessed the damage caused by a lack of focus and disconnect between employees and the company vision play out with a client. They were struggling with a mission-critical department: The team's attention to detail, commitment level, and accountability were at an all-time low. To make matters worse, this particular department had become a bottleneck for the entire company; they were not process-ing work in a timely manner and sometimes obstructed the work of other departments. People started to complain about surly and rude interactions with the staff. They were overall unhelpful and, at times, created significant roadblocks to growth for the company. Leadership assumed it was a training issue; they were wrong.

Upon investigation, we discovered no one in that particular department knew anything about the company's strategy or vision. They were pursuing their own unique agendas without regard for how their work fit in with the rest of the company. Further, the employees exhibited little or no connection to the company. When asked why they chose to work there, almost everyone responded in a similar vein: "It's close to where I live," or "There aren't a lot of jobs out here." These employees had never been connected to the company's vision or goals. They didn't understand the importance of their work in achieving the strategy, so they did not go the extra mile. Ultimately, new leadership was brought in to build a team that embraced and committed to the vision.

> **Make sure everyone knows *why* they are there and buys into that *why.***

Make sure everyone knows *why* they are there and buys into that *why*.

Strategy = the What

Strategy is a set of medium-term goals or initiatives the company intends to accomplish over a fixed period of time in pursuit of the vision. Setting strategy is a process of identifying the most important priorities, and it's usually executed at the corporate level. We highly recommend leadership teams engage with and gather input from employees, board members, and other key stakeholders. People who are expected to execute the strategy should be involved in creating it.

In the past, organizations formulated strategy every five to ten years, but the recent pace of change has accelerated the suggested time frame to every one to three years. Organizations must be nimble and ready to shift their strategic focus quickly to respond to rapidly changing market forces: rising interest rates, labor shortages, technological advances, and disruption in global supply chains, to name a few.

> **People who are expected to execute the strategy should be involved in creating it.**

To set strategy, you and your leadership team should answer the following questions:

1. What does the company need to accomplish in the next one to three years to further the vision?

2. What work will move those goals forward?

Identifying these two critical elements requires a thorough understanding of the competitive landscape, industry trends, the organization's strengths and limitations, market opportunities and threats, resources, and capabilities.

An organizational strategy consists generally of three to five high-level, measurable objectives. Keeping the number of company-wide objectives low is critical because too many leads to confusion and competing priorities. The purpose of creating a strategy is to give people clarity of direction, so don't try to bite off more than the team can chew. If the strategic objectives are confusing or overwhelming, they will need further refining.

Some examples of focused business strategies are as follows:

- Google: To accelerate innovation and strengthen brand loyalty through transformational changes while creating an open-source environment[4]
- Nike: To accelerate investment to create a truly distinctive digital experience through our own platforms[5]
- Amazon: A relentless focus on the customer, continuous innovation, operational excellence, and the ability to think long-term[6]
- Apple: To bring the best user experience to customers through innovative hardware, software, and services[7]

Strategy dictates where your organization directs its time, money, and resources. It is supported by the structure of the organization, the composition of the leadership team, the nature of talent, and the culture. And because strategy is the foundation for almost every key decision and initiative, you should frequently revisit it, particularly when circumstances change.

CASE IN POINT: STRATEGIC MISALIGNMENT

A company in Silicon Valley had pioneered a platform and revolutionized the way physicians treat their patients. The technology team was on the cutting edge of the industry, constantly innovating and improving the platform's capability. Initially, the organizational strategy was to capture as much market share as possible. To execute this strategy, they agreed to accommodate any customer-requested modifications, regardless of whether those requested features advanced the original vision and strategy.

When the company entered the Operationalize stage, it needed to standardize its products rather than continue customizing. This strategic shift wasn't clearly communicated to the sales team, who continued to promise new customized features. Meanwhile, the engineers were instructed to focus on supporting the products they had already built. The organization was moving in two directions, and technology was caught in the middle. They had conflicting priorities and could not determine which was more important. The operations were out of alignment with the vision and the strategy. Unsurprisingly, frustration and friction emerged. The constant confusion and lack of directional focus resulted in massive technical debt, strained customer relationships, angry engineers, and frazzled customer service reps. The CEO was constantly called in to referee disputes over where time and resources should be allocated.

If you're the CEO and your people constantly come to you to resolve disputes, that's a sure sign your organization lacks clarity about its strategic priorities. Ensure your strategic priorities are defined, communicated, and understood to avoid misalignment.

Goal Setting = the How

Goals are the near-term tasks the company must accomplish to support its strategy. They are the bedrock of execution, and they lay the foundation for accountability. Goals are the framework against which to measure performance and productivity. Goal setting sharpens focus by aligning the team around the most important work and by measuring the results of that work.

If your company's focus is sharp, every employee will understand the vision and the strategy, and their goals and priorities will align with both. They will understand how their work connects to the success of the overall business strategy, and they will be able to prioritize their daily tasks accordingly. Goals exist across all levels of the organization—corporate, team, and individual—and they may be set and reviewed monthly, quarterly, or annually. Ideally, each individual's goals will be cascading, which means they align with the team's goals and support the corporate strategy and vision.

CASE IN POINT: DRAW THE PLACE

Years ago, Howard was in Italy for a conference, and the facilitator had everyone think of one place they wanted to visit more than anything. After several minutes, the facilitator passed around sheets of paper and asked the group to draw the location they wanted to visit. Less than 30 seconds into the assignment, the facilitator asked everyone to stop and give their drawings to the person on their left.

The person on the left was required to prepare a detailed travel itinerary for the visit with directions, travel arrangements, a full packing list, and a list of activities. The whole group laughed when they saw the drawing they had to work with. The drawings weren't close to complete, and there wasn't enough detail in most

If your company's focus is sharp, every employee will understand the vision and the strategy, and their goals and priorities will align with both.

of the drawings to even figure out what the destination was, let alone make plans on how to get there or what would be needed.

This is often what leaders and employees experience. As CEO, you can picture the destination vividly. You can see the details, know how you will get there, and know what activities you want to do when you get there. Unless you convey your vision to the rest of the team with the same amount of detail you have in your head, it is very difficult for anyone to help you get there.

EXAMPLE OF CASCADING GOALS

Vision	Nike: To Bring Inspiration and Innovation to Every Athlete in the World
Strategy	Develop wearable technology to track athletes' heartrate and distance and launch by 2025.
Team Goal	Corporate Development Team: Complete the acquisition of a wearable tech company with strong engineering team by 6/30/24
Individual Goal	Attend 3 conferences to network with companies in wearable technology.

USE THE TOOLS: EOS AND OKRS

As the old adage goes, "You can't manage what you don't measure." Strategy alone is too ambiguous to execute without concrete, measurable goals. Two of the most effective goal-setting methods and measurement tools are EOS and OKRs. You're probably familiar with one or both of them, but we've summarized them here for a quick refresher.

EOS stands for Entrepreneurial Operating System, which is the brainchild of Gino Wickman and is outlined in his 2011 book, *Traction: Get a Grip on Your Business*. Wickman built a high-growth organization of his own around the methodology, as EOS provides a complete structure for operations including running efficient meetings, utilizing metrics, and people management.

Consultants, called "Implementers" in Wickman's world, facilitate the adoption of EOS and introduce organizations to its tools, templates, and accountability structures. Implementers generally work with an organization for up to two years to ensure the leadership teams have a firm handle on how to run the processes on their own. If your organization is struggling with clarity and accountability, and your team is hungry for tools, templates, and a guide, EOS might be the right methodology for you. Plus, it can be used for any type of business, from construction to high-growth tech start-ups.

Andy Grove, the renowned former CEO of Intel, developed the concept of OKRs—an acronym for "objectives" and "key results"— in the 1970s. The concept was later popularized by Intel alumnus and legendary tech investor John Doerr, of Kleiner Perkins. Doerr introduced the OKR methodology to many of the successful tech start-ups he advised as a board member. Famously, Google's founder Larry Page accredited OKRs with his company's "10x growth, many times over." In 2018, Doerr shared his insights in the best-selling book *Measure What Matters: How Google, Bono, and the Gates Foundation Rock the World with OKRs*. Quite simply, "objectives" are *what* you are going to accomplish, and "key results" are *how* you will accomplish those objectives. The OKR methodology emphasizes the use of measurable, time-bound goals to chart progress.

Meg used OKRs when she worked at Google in the early days. Each employee had quarterly OKRs that clearly aligned with departmental and company quarterly OKRs. The method lends itself well to technology companies and organizations that already have a culture of accountability. It's a simple yet powerful way to make goal setting consistent and visible across the organization. The most challenging part of the OKR method is setting the *right* goals. Organizations will need a few quarters of practice to get it right. Start small and start early, first with company goals among the leadership team, and then roll the process out to departments and individual employees.

Reviewing goals frequently is especially critical for high-growth companies. What you learn during the review process, both the failures and the successes, informs your strategy, people, and processes and allows you to pivot quickly when necessary. If you only review goals annually, you may lose valuable time to make a change. Whether you choose OKRs, EOS, or something else entirely, commit to your chosen method for a significant period of time (two years, minimum) to fully realize the benefits. Capitalize on the priceless knowledge of high-growth CEOs and board members who have paved the way: Gino Wickman, Andy Grove, and John Doerr.

Sharpening Focus across the Four Stages of the Growth Gauntlet

When your company has multiple opportunities and a host of Growth Gauntlet challenges, sharpening focus can be very difficult. Where should you direct your energy and resources? What is the best use of your time? Who are the ideal clients? What, exactly, is your differentiating product or service? Are you spread too thin or too wide? What are the biggest threats to your sustainability? Not to mention, *how* you go about sharpening your focus changes at each stage of the company's growth.

In the Emerge stage, the company's primary focus is on proving out a product, market, or business model (or all three). The focus revolves around the original idea or concept that led the founder to start the business. Having said that, it's not unusual for the focus to shift as test-ing, learning, and, yes, even failing, lead the team to change course. That's okay. In the Emerge stage, everything's an experiment, and the mantra is "fail fast." It's great to try lots of things, but the trick is to find something that works before your resources run out. As the experi-ments give way to a product or market with real potential, investors buy in, or revenue starts rolling in, then it's time to sharpen focus again.

In the Operationalize stage, the focus shifts to setting up the processes and structures by which the business can grow. It is charac-terized by the organization coalescing around the consistent delivery of a product or service to the clients. At this point, the organization becomes more complex when it adds more people and specialized teams, which require more pro-cesses and accountability than in the Emerge stage. To sharpen focus, it's critical to engage as many employees as possible in the work of discerning the company's vision, committing it to paper, and communicating it to the team.

If you only review goals annually, you may lose valuable time to make a change.

Employees value being a part of such foundational work, which is the launching point to galvanize the team, recruit new employees, make strategic decisions, and define your corporate identity.

The hallmark of the Thrive stage is predictability. Companies will have a goal-setting method firmly in place, along with many other systems to track and measure progress. Now, the organization can harvest data from those processes and systems to drive deci-sion-making and sharpen focus even further.

Jim Barksdale, former CEO of Netscape, famously said, "If we have data, let's look at the data. If all we have are opinions, let's go with mine." In the Emerge or the Operationalize stage, you likely won't have the complete data Jim's talking about and you'll be relegated to going with your gut. As the company moves to the Thrive stage, you'll be equipped with the numbers to override your gut and make a sound decision. And that's how you'll know when you have arrived at the Thrive stage—when you have sufficient data to make decisions.

The Explore and Expand stage requires a successful, mature business to continue its growth trajectory by taking on something new: a new geography, product line, acquisition, and so on. When these activities enter the mix, the task of sharpening focus becomes more complex, but the key is to employ the same discipline to align strategy with your vision.

CASE IN POINT: DUAL FOCUS

Several years ago, we worked with an old-line telecom company. As landlines became obsolete and internet usage surged, the business shifted to providing residential internet and cable. When growth in the residential market plateaued, the mature and stable business looked for ways to innovate.

First, the owners brought in a new CEO and gave him a mandate to evolve the company. He pursued an adjacent line of business selling fiber to commercial entities. The new business had a completely different business model, which required people with different skills and experience. It was, in effect, a start-up within a mature business.

The CEO and his new leadership team were excited about their vision for this new venture. In fact, they talked about it to employees every chance they got, by the watercooler and in town hall meetings. The problem was only about 20 percent of employees were a part of the exciting new venture. The other 80 percent were longtime employees in the mature and stable—yet decidedly less sexy—part of the business, the part that accounted for 90 percent of revenue. They did not see themselves in the new vision. These employees started to feel there would no longer be a place for them at the company. They felt betrayed and began to leave the company.

In reality, the mature business was critical to the company's long-term success. The new line of business would not be profitable for some time. By sharpening the focus only on the shiny, new, innovative part of the business, the CEO neglected the profitable heart and soul of the company.

Once the CEO understood the problem, he was able to create two visions and two very different sets of goals: one for the mature business and one for the start-up. The mature business set goals around harvesting efficiencies and making small changes to retain customers and steadily grow market share. The start-up set goals more similar to those in the Emerge stage. They focused on moving quickly to build products and establish a beachhead in the marketplace. The two entities were resourced differently based on the dual focus. Employees were recognized and rewarded for efficiency on one side of the business and for innovation and growth on the other.

Under the new dual vision, every employee could see themselves in the vision, no matter where they sat in the company, and could clearly understand how their daily work contributed to the overall success of the company. The CEO understood the vision, strategy, and goals for each line of business needed to be vastly different, which dictated the talent required for each (his own included).

Don't attempt to survive the Growth Gauntlet without a clear understanding of what you want to achieve. Vision, strategy, and goals form the foundation of an accountability structure for execution. With these critical elements in place to guide the work, you can proceed with clarity and confidence. Tough decisions or unforeseen crossroads are your opportunity to return to the vision (to seek guidance), to the strategy (to work the plan), and to the goals (to measure progress). These three core elements within the Sharpen Focus Imperative are your North Star. They map out the intended route to get there and identify your directional mileposts along the way.

Leveling Up: The Strategic Edge

Critical Questions for the CEO to Ask

1. Does the company have a clear vision and strategy?

2. Are my employees connected to the vision of the company?

3. Does my leadership team understand and are they aligned around the top three to five priorities of the business?

4. Where does friction exist in the organization, and could it be the result of competing priorities?

5. Do we need to up our game on accountability by adding a goal-setting framework?

6. Does each member of the leadership team have clear goals and objectives aligned with the corporate strategy?

Critical Questions for the Board to Ask

1. Is the CEO able to clearly articulate the vision and strategy of the company?

2. Are there measurable goals in place to track progress on the strategy?

3. Are time and resources appropriately allocated to the strategic priorities of the business?

4. Is there anything/anyone distracting time and resources from the strategic priorities?

5. Is there any part of the business that is not aligned with the strategy?

Milestones and Initiatives

- Establish and champion a clear vision.
- Establish a strategic-planning process.
- Establish a goal-setting process for the company, each department, and each individual.
- Measure progress at regular intervals.

Sharpen Focus Quick Reference

Stages of Growth			
Emerge Informal, Ad Hoc, Undefined, Reactive	**Operationalize** Defined, Data-Informed, Focused, Proactive	**Thrive** Accountable, Data-Driven, Predictable	**Explore & Expand** Strategic, Agile, Innovative, Opportunistic
Primary focus is on proving out product, market, or business model.	Product, market, or business model is proven. Stated corporate purpose/vision exists. The focus is mostly on achieving revenue goals. A goal-setting framework is introduced.	Detailed Strategic Plan exists with budgets, forecasts, and data-driven metrics. Focus is on growing market share. Corporate and individual goals in place.	Business is regularly meeting financial targets. With operations running smoothly, the focus shifts from internal operations to exploring external opportunities. Dual innovation occurs.

What is it?

- Vision
- Strategy
- Goal Setting

What's the value?

Vision, strategy, and goals define the direction and establish *what* work will be accomplished. Setting goals aligns the team and allows for tracking and measuring progress.

CHAPTER 3

Calibrate Culture

"If you do not manage culture, it manages you."

—Edgar Schein, *Organizational Culture and Leadership*

"MINNESOTA NICE" is the way employees described the culture of the tech firm they worked for. "You know, everyone is just really nice. The culture is great. Very collegial." Sounds great, right? But there was a downside to Minnesota nice. People were so focused on being nice they found it difficult to hold their good friends accountable for results, at least openly. It translated to a highly relational culture with an aversion to tough conversations. Relationship currency was a key decision driver over the more objective data and processes.

This emphasis on nice relationships had worked and was even a badge of honor in the early days of the start-up, but as the company grew, the need for accountability and open dissent increased. The passive and always outwardly positive Minnesota nice culture was getting in the way of growth. When your focus changes, your culture needs to evolve to support it. Sometimes, it's a wholesale change, but most often, it's a recalibration of certain aspects of the culture to align with the new direction.

In high-growth companies, culture is often viewed in a different category than strategy. In fact, the concept of culture is mistaken for overall morale, the level of employee engagement, and retention rates. To be sure, culture impacts those things, but to view culture solely through the lens of employee happiness is to overlook its most critical and important potential—helping the company achieve the intended results as set forth in the strategy.

Culture can be either a catalyst or a constraint.

Culture can be either a catalyst or a constraint for reaching your goals and achieving your desired results. If your culture is not aligned with your business goals, it's a constraint, and you will be hard-pressed to get anything done, no matter how brilliant your strategy or implementation plan may be.

What Is Culture?

For all the importance and attention the topic of culture has gained in recent years, experts still find it difficult to agree on a definition. Since it came into executive consciousness in the late 1980s and early '90s, thousands of books have been written about organizational culture. Edgar Schein, the renowned professor at MIT Sloan School of Management and widely considered grandfather of organizational culture, describes culture as having three components: artifacts, espoused values, and underlying assumptions.[8]

1. Artifacts are the visible organizational structures, processes, and behaviors of leaders and employees. A new employee can generally identify and observe organizational artifacts quickly.

2. Espoused values are the organization's values, strategies, goals, and philosophies. These are often on a wall somewhere.

3. Underlying assumptions are team members' unconscious beliefs, perceptions, thoughts, and actions that contribute to the actual values, decision-making framework, and choice of actions.

Ultimately, organizational culture influences, and is influenced by, who is hired, how business is conducted, how decisions are made, what work is prioritized, and what aspects of performance are rewarded. It is connected to the beliefs and experiences employees share and which values and "rules of the road" are passed down to new employees both through formal culture training and informal stories. Culture governs *how* work gets done and *why* employees make the decisions and take the actions they do.

Culture's importance to and impact on an organization's success was succinctly captured by Peter Drucker in his famous declaration, "Culture eats strategy for breakfast." David Cummings, co-founder of Pardot, said, "Corporate culture is the only sustainable competitive advantage that is completely within the control of the entrepreneur."[9] Former IBM chairman Louis Gerstner put a finer point on it: "Culture isn't just one aspect of the game—*it is the game*."[10]

Early in the life cycle of a company, the CEO is either making all of the decisions or is part of the decision-making process. As a company grows, there is no way for the CEO to be part of every decision or to be present every time someone else makes a decision. But, ultimately, he or she is still responsible for those decisions. This is where culture comes into play because you want to make sure decisions and actions are consistent with the company's vision and values. Serial entrepreneur and investor Ben Horowitz has this to say: "Your culture is how your company makes decisions when you're not there. It's the set of assumptions your employees use to resolve the problems they face every day. It's how they behave when no one is looking."[11] Or, as we like to say, culture is the boss when the boss is not around.

Culture is the boss when the boss is not around.

CASE IN POINT: CULTURE AS THE BOSS

In the early 2000s, Google's co-founder Larry Page was notoriously focused on hiring, and he maintained a high standard for adding talent to the organization. His philosophy was if you put a bunch of exceptionally bright talented people together, then brilliant ideas will spontaneously combust. Winning on talent became a key strategy for Google.

In his pursuit of top talent, Larry developed a strong internal committee system. He made it clear to everyone in the company that they had a role to play in hiring. Those roles included sourcing, referring candidates, interviewing, sitting on hiring committees, and training new hires, who were known as "nooglers."

Candidates routinely interviewed with eight to ten individual employees. Each interviewer input their feedback and scores into an applicant tracking system. The feedback was then aggregated into a hiring packet and reviewed by the hiring committee. The group decided whether to move a candidate forward in the process or not. If a candidate was to move forward, the hiring packet was forwarded to Larry Page for final approval.

When Meg was at Google, the company hired over 100 people per week. So, it would be natural to assume that Larry's review of the packet was merely a formality, but not so! Stories quickly circulated about Larry calling interviewers in the middle of the night for clarity on a comment or a score related to a particular candidate. He was known for sending hiring packets back to the committees to ask for more information or, worse, to override their decision and reject the candidate outright.

As a result, Google employees took their role as interviewers quite seriously. They asked the questions they knew Larry would want answers to and gathered the information they anticipated he would want to know. Though Larry was not physically sitting in on each interview, his rigorous commitment to hiring only the best talent was top of mind for the interviewers. In a very literal sense, the hiring culture he created was the boss when he wasn't around.

Whose Responsibility Is Culture?

For a company in the Emerge stage, the CEO is usually the architect of the culture, either intentionally or unwittingly. Many times, the culture develops as an extension of the founder's own values, personality, and expectations.

One of the most notable examples of this is Steve Jobs. His passion for design, which set Apple apart from other technology companies from the get-go, has continued long after his death. Another notable example on the negative side is Uber's notoriously ethically flexible former CEO, Travis Kalanick. After his hasty departure in the midst of a scandal, the entire company culture needed a reboot to recover from the toxicity his leadership instilled.[12]

As a company grows and matures, its culture must exist independently of the founder. The CEO must drive the culture, which is certainly the case during the Emerge stage. In this early stage, there is typically a "felt sense" of the culture, but it is not necessarily defined in a formal manner. Yet, as the company evolves and grows, culture must become a key pillar of its organizational strategy.

By default, a founder CEO is the company's first chief culture officer. As the leader of leaders, the CEO must embody, reinforce, and hold the line on the culture. In addition, the CEO must actively build, manage, and steward the culture by making it a key part of every strategic plan. It is paramount for leadership to set the example for everyone else to follow because when a CEO acts in ways that are contrary to the culture—like flying first class, showing up late to the office, or disrespecting team members—those new behaviors rewrite the rules for everyone.

It can be challenging for a CEO to spend the time needed to drive the culture, especially in a growing business when everyone is working at full capacity. As a result, it can be tempting as a CEO to outsource its management to HR. While HR is an important business partner in implementing culture across the different employee processes it owns, HR cannot be successful unless its actions are fully endorsed, supported, and actively promoted by the leadership team. If the CEO is the chief culture officer, HR is the culture reinforcement team, taking direction from the top and infusing the culture into the employee life cycle processes.

Middle managers also have a huge role to play in stewarding the culture as the organization grows. We like to think of them as the culture disciples who have been anointed by the leaders to evangelize the culture to the farthest reaches of the organization. As the company grows and the leadership team can no longer interact with each employee, the middle management group becomes an important army of culture ambassadors to train employees and hold them accountable for living into the culture.

What Makes Culture "Good"?

Over the past two decades, there has been an increased focus and effort on building good corporate cultures, but it's not a one-size-fits-all endeavor. Edgar Schein draws a contrast between a "good" and "effective" culture. Many leaders are focused on whether they have a good culture. Do we have enough perks or recognition programs or events to qualify as a good culture? Schein offers that the measure of an organization's culture should be whether it is effective in helping that organization achieve its goals or resolve its problems. There is no single, universally accepted definition of a "good" culture.

Effective cultures vary widely, and what is effective for one organization may not be for another. For example, the command-and-control, hierarchical culture of the US Army helps them accomplish their strategic objectives. At the other end of the spectrum, Google's collaborative culture and relatively flat structure are conducive to innovation. If you switched the cultures of the US Army and Google for a week, disaster would ensue.

Sometime in the early 1990s, in an effort to attract and retain top talent, corporations started adding a wide range of amenities to their workplaces, some more outlandish than others. We saw the rise of the corporate café and the fitness center, premier parking, and table tennis. A tour of Bloomberg's Manhattan headquarters in the '90s included a spin through their beautiful new employee kitchen, which was stocked with every kind of breakfast cereal and assorted free snacks and drinks. On the West Coast, many start-ups in the tech industry promoted an on-site masseuse and free beer Fridays. The amenities came to define whether a culture was "good." It was generally assumed amenities were corporate perks invented to lure talent. But the reality is many perks had a strategic purpose.

Tech companies wanted to create an atmosphere that fulfilled the engineers' every need to the degree they would never have to leave "campus" for anything. People were incentivized to prolong their workdays with minimal interruption, which is why their meals and snacks were free. Regular on-site massages guarded against carpel tunnel and the orthopedic hazards of sitting for extended periods in front of a computer screen. Free beers on Fridays lured employees to all-hands meetings where important announcements were made. And eventually, shuttle buses to and from downtown San Francisco included free Wi-Fi, which extended the workday into the commute time. All of these so-called perks contributed to a culture of greater productivity (like it or not). At the Silicon Valley tech companies, the culture supported the strategy.

The Three Ds: Define, Demonstrate, and Defend

Culture building has undergone much iteration over the last few decades. These days, the tech-style amenities of the '90s are more widely recognized for what they were: a way to keep people at work and working as long as possible. In our work with high-growth companies, we've discovered there are three key steps to creating a world-class sustainable culture that outlasts employment trends: define, demonstrate, and defend.

1. DEFINE

As your company grows and you begin to position the culture to stand on its own, the first step is to define it. All organizations have a culture. The key is discovering what it actually is and then defining it in the form of core values that will propel your strategy. Jim Collins and Jerry Porras wrote the seminal work on core vision and values called "Building Your Company's Vision," published in 1996 in the *Harvard Business Review*. According to Collins and Porras, "Core values are the handful of guiding principles by which a company navigates." Defining core values is a group exercise because people experience the culture in different ways across the organization.

Companies must take a multipronged approach to discover and define their core values. First, review the artifacts: the website, the strategic plan, and the marketing materials. Who does the company say it is? What values are conveyed to employees and customers? Next, interview and/or survey as many stakeholders as possible to discover what values exist. Observe leadership meetings, town halls, and corporate celebrations to see what values are present, how the people interact with one another, and how decisions are made.

Bring all of your insights from the culture due diligence to the leadership team for an off-site to define the most important five to seven core values evident in the company. Don't go overboard listing ten or more core values. People can really only remember five to seven. To free up space on your list, avoid "table stakes" values, which are basic human characteristics any employee must have to pass the hiring bar, such as "Integrity." Don't waste precious real estate by citing values that are (hopefully) a given.

In addition to the five to seven guiding values, you may want to identify aspirational values. These might be values that are not currently ingrained across the organization but will eventually be necessary for the company to level up and achieve its strategy. As companies move through the Four Stages of the Growth Gauntlet, the culture will evolve. For example, leadership teams often say they want the culture to "embrace using data to drive decision-making." When the company is in the Emerge stage, it may not have the systems in place to capture data regularly and consistently to support decisions. Adding those systems and formalizing the processes of using data may come later, in the Operationalize stage. During the Emerge stage, we might say "using data to drive decisions" is an *aspirational* core value that will likely be realized and become a core value at a later stage.

Critically, your list of values must clearly set you apart from other companies. Think about it this way: If someone read your list of values, would they be able to identify your company? They should accurately represent what you stand for, strive for, and live by, which is why values are more than just words on a poster in the lobby. They provide a framework and a guide for decision-making.

CASE IN POINT: CREATING HAPPINESS

In its early days, Disneyland used an effective practice to communicate the importance of its core value, customer service, during its "cast member" orientation. The overriding vision of the organization is "We Create Happiness," and no matter what your role is in the park, you are responsible for making guests happy. It doesn't matter if you're Mickey Mouse, the person spinning cotton candy, or the guy collecting tickets. Creating happiness is driven by a set of values designed both to indoctrinate employees into the Disneyland culture

> **Values are more than just words on a poster in the lobby.**

and to operationalize how cast members should carry out their happiness mission.

The Disneyland recipe for creating happiness is expressed as four simple core values:[13]

1. Safety

2. Courtesy

3. Show

4. Efficiency

The four values outline a decision-making framework for employees to follow when interacting with guests. And the order of the values is deliberate. Safety first. Always. It's impossible to feel happy if you don't feel safe. Next is "Courtesy," followed by "Show." "Show" is a value unique to Disney. When Meg and her family visited the park in Orlando, they stayed at the Animal Kingdom resort. When they returned to their room each night, the bath towels and washcloths were meticulously formed into elaborate origami animals. And finally, because make no mistake, Disney is a business, the value of "Efficiency" is demonstrated through the careful and calculated manner in which the park directs and transports large crowds of people.

Imagine how the guiding vision and the set of four core values come into play if someone drops a Coke bottle on Main Street, USA. A cast member dressed as a chimney sweep rushes to the aid of the guest. He establishes a safety perimeter so the broken glass won't impact other guests. Then, he sweeps the glass away while doing his best impression of Dick Van Dyke and singing, "Chim chiminey, chim chiminey, chim chim cher-ee." What a show! The cast member knows how to respond to the situation because of the framework, and the guests forget all about broken glass because they are enjoying the "show." Magic.

2. DEMONSTRATE

Once a company defines its core values, it's time to indoctrinate employees and live into the values. There are many opportunities to reinforce culture. Leaders model the culture by what they prioritize and how they manage. Processes and communications provide opportunities to reinforce culture, too. Each step within the cycle is an opportunity to illustrate how the values are practiced. For example, you can (and should) use the processes associated with the employee life cycle—from hiring to training to performance management—to reinforce culture.

RECRUITING

Ensure people are steeped in the culture from the first moment of contact. Screening for culture fit on the front end of the interview process boosts your likelihood of hiring and retaining the right people. Make sure your culture comes through loud and clear on your website and in your job postings and job descriptions. Some companies use personality screening assessments such as the Predictive Index and Culture Index to determine early in the process whether a candidate is a likely match for the company.

> **Use the processes associated with the employee life cycle—from hiring to training to performance management—to reinforce culture.**

HIRING

Candidates see your values in action when they interact with your employees. Train interviewers to talk about your culture and give examples of how it feels to work in the organization. Develop behavioral interview questions around each of your core values to probe for evidence on how the candidate would function in your unique culture.

ONBOARDING

Most companies focus solely on operational orientation, like making sure a new hire has a desk and an email address and knows where the restrooms are. Go the extra mile and take the time to indoctrinate people into the values and the culture. Lay out the expectations for new employees about where they should expect to see core values in action.

TRAINING AND DEVELOPMENT

Even long-tenured employees need to be reminded of the culture from time to time. Whether it's safety, leadership, or anti-harassment training, there is always an opportunity to reinforce culture in the curriculum. Make explicit connections for people so they link the concepts to the values. For example, if your core values include respect for others, anti-harassment training can be framed as explicitly linked to that core value.

REWARD SYSTEMS

What you reward speaks volumes about your values. Reward systems include performance management, compensation and benefits, employee recognition programs, and even titling and promotion practices. Each of these rewards reinforces behaviors the company values, so be sure what you are promoting aligns with the company's values. If teamwork and collaboration are key elements of the culture, then rewarding individuals with large bonuses signals that the organization is out of step with its values.

DECISION-MAKING

Core values act as a decision-making guide. It's helpful to frame tough decisions in terms of the agreed-upon core values. What does our culture suggest we should do in this instance? If we make X decision, are we violating our culture? Employees who default to these types of questions change the game.

INTERNAL COMMUNICATION

Frequent communication is an important vehicle for reinforcing culture. Email announcements, town halls, and regular staff meetings create opportunities to demonstrate culture. For internal publications or town halls, include a culture story featuring an employee who exemplified the values in their work or a testimonial from a customer who experienced your values in action, like excellent customer service. In staff meetings, kick things off with a short culture minute. Assign an employee to give a brief overview of one of the core values and share how it influences their work.

BRANDING AND MARKETING

No one likes a hypocrite. The face you show to the world must be aligned with your internal culture. Smart branding professionals start with internal values and culture and build a consistent outward brand. They revisit that alignment from time to time to ensure the internal and external values and culture do not drift away from one another.

THE BUILT ENVIRONMENT (OFFICE SPACE)

What does your office say about who you are? Do you say you're collaborative, but everyone has an individual office with a closed door? How can the physical space be designed or adapted to reflect and reinforce your culture? Design the physical space to reflect your values. If you value collaboration, have lots of spaces for groups to gather. If you value equity over hierarchy, perhaps you will have many identical workspaces for employees versus tiered workspaces allocated based on hierarchy.

3. DEFEND

Toyota is known for its values and culture. Books have been written about the Toyota Way. Several years ago, Howard was on a panel with executives from AT&T, Delta, and Toyota and heard the story of how Toyota defended its culture by holding the line on its values in hiring decisions even when it hurt revenue.

Toyota was in the middle of centralizing its operations in Plano, Texas, and was faced with the need to hire thousands of employees. Toyota unapologetically used its values and culture in the hiring process to determine whether candidates were a good fit. Many were not, which caused the already huge task to take even longer. Faced with the possibility of having to push back the opening of its new headquarters, Toyota did not waver in its commitment to its culture and values. They continued to demonstrate and defend their values and culture in every interview—accepting the significant but short-term business disruption in exchange for maintaining their culture—a critical piece of their competitive advantage.

Once your culture is established, it must be defended at all costs. What does this mean? It means when something or someone challenges or threatens your culture, you must stand firm and protect it from the saboteurs. Cultural threats usually come in the form of people who are not aligned with the company's vision and values, which is why you need to pay vigilant attention to people's behaviors and attitudes. And be aware that misalignment can occur at any level.

CASE IN POINT: MERGING LEADERSHIP

Several years ago, four small companies merged to create one larger business. Each company had its own founder and culture, but the leadership knew they would have to create a single unified organization to succeed. For several years, the company grew and prospered. But there was a problem. One of the original founders was not culturally aligned with the others. He created a toxic work environment for employees, some of whom left the company. Though the others tried their best to help him change his behavior, he would not bend. Finally, they made the wise but painful decision to exit him from the business.

Certainly, the decision to exit a key founder came at a significant cost: lost revenue from a big producer, broken relationships, intellectual capital, and so on. But there was also a cost to enduring behavior antithetical to what the company aspired to be. They wanted to be an organization where employees could trust leadership to do the right thing, and they wanted their culture and values to be more than just lip service. In the end, they were not willing to compromise their culture simply because one leader brought in significant revenue. This tough decision proved to be a critical inflection point for the company. Revenue, culture, and morale improved. Critically, they were able to live into the more unified "one company" culture, and they never looked back.

One of our favorite maxims is "Culture is the worst behavior you are willing to tolerate," which comes from authors Steve Gruenert and Todd Whitaker's 2015 book, *School Culture Rewired.* Establishing cultural norms is a lot like parenting. With a toddler, you set firm boundaries. For most parents, the toddler eventually wears you down. You let the rules slide and indulge them by letting them stay up late or have dessert before bedtime. If you've ever experienced this, you know it's hard to reinstate the boundary once it has been crossed. The same is true in the corporate world.

Tolerating bad behavior or behavior that is inconsistent with your culture will lead your company in an unintended direction and have an adverse effect on the rest of the team. We often see organizations tolerating bad behavior when revenue is at stake from big producers, long-tenured employees, and family members working in the business. Those types of relationships, with people who operate as untouchable, can cloud a leader's judgment and wreak havoc throughout the rest of the company.

CASE IN POINT: RED FLAGS

Years ago, Meg worked with a team performing due diligence on an acquisition. She did some backdoor referencing of the target's leadership, and the feedback she received was chilling. In her entire career, it was the only time she raised her hand and definitively said, "We should not do this deal based on the character of the two founders." She was overruled. The team argued in favor of the deal's economics and the opportunity.

About 18 months later, post-integration, the negative behaviors Meg heard about in the diligence process began to surface. The win-at-all-costs mentality, the condescending attitudes, and a shocking lack of integrity raised red flags and caused friction between the rest of the team and the highly collaborative, idealistic, meritocratic acquirer.

Eventually, and ironically, Meg was sent to terminate the two founders. The whole thing ended in a long and costly legal battle that far outweighed the benefits of the initial acquisition. It was ugly. And it could have been avoided if the acquiring company had paid more attention to their own organization's culture and made the tough decision to defend it by passing on the acquisition.

Tension vs. Friction

A strong and effective culture will permeate decisions and actions. It will attract and retain those in alignment and, in most cases, serve as a repellent to those who do not share the same values. A healthy tension exists (or should exist) in all organizations. Sales will always be pushing Product and Engineering's buttons. The risk management side of the house will always push back on the risk-taking side of the house. Healthy tension, open dissent, and good, solid arguments are necessary to get the best outcome for the business. But friction is another story.

CASE IN POINT: CULTURAL DISSONANCE

Meg once sat on a board that just made her angry. Every single meeting rubbed her the wrong way. There was a closely held power group that seemed to make all the decisions without discussion or consent of the full board. There were "meetings before the meetings" and "meetings after the meetings" where the real business took place. People were afraid to speak up about issues that bothered them or challenge the power group in front of the whole board.

Seeking insight on how to handle the situation, Meg shared her frustration with her coach. Her coach listened and then dispensed some unforgettable wisdom. "This board is not the right cultural fit for you." She reminded Meg of her own values: collaboration and transparency. She said it was unlikely Meg would ever thrive in a culture that didn't share the same values. She explained the friction Meg was experiencing was the result of the cultural dissonance between her values and the organization's. And then, she gave Meg "permission" to resign. A huge weight was lifted, and she did not waste any time extricating herself. Now, whenever she is tempted to join an organization, she does thorough cultural due diligence to ensure the organization is a good match.

Measuring Culture's Effectiveness

How do you measure something as intangible as culture? To assess the likely effectiveness of your current culture, ask yourself and your leadership team this: If everyone continues to think and act the way they do, will we be able to achieve the results we want?

This question is challenging to ask at any stage, but when a company is nearing or entering a new stage of growth, the answer is often "No" or "Absolutely not!" If that's the case, you need to calibrate your culture to align with and support the direction you're going and the results you want. Regardless, changing the culture is hard. Culture is like a huge ocean liner dragging an anchor. It takes concentrated intention and effort to make any change.

> **If everyone continues to think and act the way they do, will we be able to achieve the results we want?**

In calibrating your culture to your sharpened focus, you first want to determine whether you're meeting your goals and getting the results you want. If you are, then your culture is effective. The results do not only have to equate to numerical growth or revenue targets. Some of the desired results may be subjective and relate to engagement or morale. In this case, we recommend the following test questions to determine if your culture is helping you achieve those goals.

ARE WE WHO WE SAY WE ARE?

Stated core values are the way we describe our culture. We recommend asking employees periodically how well the company is living into its stated values. For example, one of our clients has the following core value: "We create customers for life." So, we asked employees to tell us to what degree they agreed with the statement. Based on the employee responses, the company had some room for improvement on this core value. By surveying employees annually on the values, leaders remind people what is important and glean useful information on where they need to spend some time to reinforce their values.

WHERE ARE WE WITH EMPLOYEE ENGAGEMENT?

Employee engagement surveys are an important way to measure morale. The most effective ones we've used include a Net Promoter Score (NPS) question. Originally developed for marketing purposes to gauge the likelihood of whether a customer would refer the product or service to someone else, a high NPS means a customer is satisfied with their experience with the company. As of late, companies are asking employees—on a scale of 1–10—whether they would refer a friend or colleague to the company as a great place to work. Generally, the higher the NPS, the healthier the culture. The NPS trend over time tends to be more interesting than one score in isolation, and asking people to comment on why they gave the score they did can help management understand what is working well or whether it needs to head off trouble.

Scrappy Culture vs. Scarcity Culture

Many emerging businesses pride themselves on running lean. Small teams accomplish a lot and "punch above their weight," but the early stage of an organization's growth is just that—a stage. Running lean becomes a problem when it morphs into a permanent way of life instead of a temporary state.

A few years ago, we spent some time with an organization that was stuck. They were functioning and meeting their basic needs, but they were not growing. As we met with several members of their team and dug into the culture, people said things like, "Oh, that would be great, but we can't afford it," or "We just don't have enough capacity to take that on," or "We can barely do all the things we have to do."

When we facilitated a team meeting to get the group energized about their future, we found they were simply unable to think big. The culture of scarcity had crippled their ability to innovate and think beyond their scarce resources. Their constant fear of running out of money created "short-termism." They were making decisions out of fear, spending money on small and near-term Band-Aids, rather than making bigger bets on longer-term solutions that would fuel growth. Getting the organization back into a growth mode required new leadership, a new vision, new funding, and many changes to the staff. The new energy and renewed focus on a longer time horizon inspired the growth that was needed. As we discovered, there is a fine but bright line between a positive and motivating culture of scrappiness and a debilitating culture of scarcity.

A Culture of Belonging and Uniqueness

Work is a human endeavor, and it is generally something done in collaborative relationships with others. Our core belief is that people drive results. To get people to do their best work, leaders must provide an environment that allows, and even compels, people to thrive.

Maslow's hierarchy of needs lays out the definitive framework for what conditions must be met for humans to achieve self-actualization. After the basic needs of food, clothing, and shelter, Maslow says people also must feel like they belong. According to Gallup, the number one predictor of employee engagement and retention is whether or not an employee has a friend at work.[14] Connecting with others is a fundamental human need. Building strong, authentic relationships with team members and interacting with others is paramount to the success of companies of any size.

But there's a catch. Employees not only want to belong; they also want to be valued for their uniqueness—the perspectives, skills, and abilities that set them apart from others. They want to be treated as insiders—allowed and encouraged to retain their uniqueness—and feel safe to be and express themselves. We believe a culture of belonging and uniqueness is what allows people to thrive.

Creating a culture of belonging requires intention and effort. It's critical to listen to employees first, to gain their perspective, and to understand what's working and what isn't. Leaders can facilitate listening through surveys, interviews, and focus groups. Feedback from those types of focused sessions helps leadership to develop a plan with specific goals that can be measured over time. HR can be a great partner in this endeavor, but the CEO and other key leaders must buy in and take the lead if the initiatives are to be successful.

Calibrating Culture across the Four Stages of the Growth Gauntlet

A healthy culture will evolve and change in support of the business strategy. When you move between the Four Stages of the Growth Gauntlet, strategic goals and desired results become more complex and challenging.

In the Emerge stage, culture is often derived directly from the founder's personality and way of doing things. Employees are indoctrinated into the culture through direct and frequent exposure to that founder. The team develops ways of working together in those early days that will later be hard coded into the organizational culture. There is a felt sense of culture, but it is not explicitly defined.

As the team grows, it becomes impossible for everyone to work closely with the founder (or founders) and to receive their culture directly from the leaders. In the Operationalize stage, the culture needs to be institutionalized so it can live outside of the people who created it. To do that, the culture must be discovered and defined. We use the term "discover" because all organizations have a culture, but many have not taken the time to memorialize it. Generally, "defining" culture means establishing a set of core values that describe the culture to push forward your strategic goals.

As the organization moves into the Thrive stage, it will add new employees and will need to be intentional about how to instill culture in those employees so the culture does not become diluted or changed unintentionally. Also, at this point, aspirational values may come into play. For example, if growth is the strategy, instilling a sales, business development, or customer service culture can be a game changer.

And finally, at the Explore and Expand stage, culture takes a front-row seat in strategic decision-making. A strong culture becomes the litmus test for key executive hires, acquisition targets, and strategic partnerships.

Core values may evolve over a company's lifespan, but they are not likely to change completely. That's why we call this imperative *calibrate* culture. "To calibrate" implies making change through small, precise movements.

Leveling Up: The Strategic Edge

Critical Questions for the CEO to Ask

1. Do our core values uniquely describe us?

2. If everyone continues to think and act the way they do, will we be able to achieve the results we want?

3. Does our brand align with our core values?

4. Does our compensation and reward system align with our core values?

5. Are there decisions that require us to defend our culture?

6. Are there any aspirational values we need to add to achieve our strategy? For example, do we need to up our game with regard to

accountability? Making data-driven decisions? Providing excellent customer service? Focusing on continuous improvement?

7. Are revenue, loyalty, or relationships clouding our judgment or causing us to tolerate behavior that is not aligned with our values?

Critical Questions for the Board to Ask

1. Is the CEO aligned with the culture of the organization?

2. Is the board aligned with the organization's culture? Is the board embracing the same culture and values it expects of the company?

3. Does the board routinely consult the values of the company when making strategic decisions?

4. Does friction exist that might signal cultural misalignment?

5. How will the board reinforce the company's culture in its committee work?

6. What indicators will the board review annually to assess the strength and effectiveness of the company's culture (employee engagement survey results, retention data, etc.)?

Milestones and Initiatives

The Growth Gauntlet lays out a path for building culturally aligned employee processes as a company scales. We recommend working in 12-month increments to focus on methodically achieving these initiatives and milestones.

Celebrate Key Milestones

- Defining core values
- Reinforcing core values through the employee life cycle
- Implementing culture training for all new hires
- Establishing a set of cultural competencies against which to evaluate new-hire candidates
- Incorporating cultural competencies into your employee performance management process
- Recognizing people for their contributions to upholding the culture at town hall meetings

Calibrate Culture Quick Reference

Stages of Growth			
Emerge Informal, Ad Hoc, Undefined, Reactive	**Operationalize** Defined, Data-Informed, Focused, Proactive	**Thrive** Accountable, Data-Driven, Predictable	**Explore & Expand** Strategic, Agile, Innovative, Opportunistic
Culture is organic, emerging, and is largely a reflection of the personality and priorities of the founder(s).	Culture moves beyond the founder. It is defined in the form of core values and used in some decision-making.	Culture is reinforced through processes like hiring, talent development, performance management, and compensation.	Culture is a driver and used as a lens through which to evaluate strategic opportunities. Culture is defended.

What is it?

- Core Values
- Behaviors
- Beliefs
- Artifacts
- Stories

What's the value?

Culture governs *how* work gets done. It is a competitive differentiator in that it is difficult to replicate. It must be defined, demonstrated, and defended at all cost.

CHAPTER 4

Strengthen Leadership

"Leadership is the capacity to translate a vision into reality."
—Warren Bennis

AN ENTREPRENEURIAL CEO generated a lot of excitement around his ideas when he launched his company, which is not uncommon. He secured early growth equity funding to scale the business but hit a tough patch when it came to building out operations. On a coaching call, we asked him to describe his ideal role and where he thought he could add the most value to the business. He said he saw himself as the captain of the ship. While he was on deck looking at the horizon and navigating, he needed a capable team of people to operate the vessel. The only problem was he hadn't built the ship yet. He didn't realize it, but he was still on dry land. The ship was still an idea. He didn't need a team of operators; he needed a shipbuilder.

This CEO was a first-class innovator—an ideas guy—and he knew his industry inside and out. He was a highly relational and inspirational person who had no trouble getting investors, clients, and employees to believe in his vision. What he lacked, though, was the experience, skills, and interest to build the mechanism to execute on his vision. His best chance for strengthening his leadership was to hire a good COO who had these strengths.

The CEO's role changes as a company moves through the Four Stages of the Growth Gauntlet. We'll explore the specifics of how the role evolves at the end of this chapter, but the necessity for strong leadership remains a constant. Whether that leadership comes from a visionary founder, an executive team, a board of directors, or a combination of all the above, an organization's success is directly tied to the strength of its leadership. Successful CEOs make it a priority to grow in their ability to lead themselves, lead others, and lead the company's strategy.

Leading Yourself

Before you can lead and strengthen your leadership team, you must first be a strong leader. How do you become a person others will follow, whose leadership helps your organization thrive? It starts with deep self-awareness of your strengths and gaps. There are numerous ways to gain such knowledge:

- Leadership assessments

- Personality and work-style assessments

- Performance feedback from your leadership team and employees

- Feedback from mentors and trusted advisors

- A leadership coach

- Self-reflection on where you thrive and what energizes you

There are lots of leadership, aptitude, and personality assessments to choose from. Myers-Briggs, DISC, Enneagram, YouScience, and CliftonStrengths are some of the most common and most easily accessible. The more you know about yourself, the better a leader you can and will be. You will understand the conditions in which you work best, seek out appropriately aligned opportunities, and build teams that complement and enhance your performance.

Whenever we interview CEO candidates, we ask about their strengths. And once we understand what those are, we ask the candidate, "Who is the first person you will hire, the person who complements your skill set and covers your blind spots and gaps?" Truly self-aware candidates will have an answer at the ready for this question. They've already thought about it because they've lived it. The answers are not as important as their self-awareness and ability to build a complete and effective team.

Some CEO candidates will say they need a top-notch CFO, someone who is deep in the numbers and can be relied on to make data-driven financial decisions. Others might need a highly relational and goal-driven VP of sales to complement their operational skill set. The most important thing is to make sure the person we're interviewing understands their own limitations and has the wherewithal and humility to place staff around them who will fill in the gaps.

STRENGTHEN YOUR IMPACT: LEAD BY EXAMPLE

CEOs are called upon to be the standard-bearer for the organization's culture. They must understand, embrace, and live the culture as they set the example for others to follow.

When Meg worked for a tech start-up in California, the emerging company hired its first non-founder CEO. The culture of the lean start-up was scrappy: class-C office space, a young team of 20-somethings, and everyone underpaid relative to their value. They were all betting on a big payoff from their equity one day. So, when the new CEO came in on his first day and requested a reserved parking spot for his cherry-red Porsche 911, it was the first alarm bell to signal this was not the right guy.

By contrast, a private equity firm hired a CEO into a turnaround situation where money was tight, and future funding was not guaranteed. The CEO lived in a different state, which forced him to commute to work by plane and stay for a couple of weeks each time. To get the message across to the rest of the team that money was tight, he told them to think about each nickel they spent as a manhole cover. To reinforce this message, he slept on a cot in his office when he was in town so as not to waste money on a hotel.

The first CEO did not make it a year. The second CEO turned the company around. He understood the power of setting a strong example. Although these stories represent extremes, it's important to think about how your behaviors set the tone for others to follow. You cannot expect others to do what you will not.

UNDERSTANDING YOUR IMPACT:
THE SHADOW OF A LEADER

In the early stages of a company, founder CEOs have more of a peer-like dynamic with their employees than that of a boss. Everyone is working around the clock to make the business work, and relationships are often personal and informal.

As the company grows and new employees join, the structure becomes more hierarchical, and there is more distance between the CEO and frontline employees. While founder CEOs no longer have the same relationships and proximity to these employees, they are still the same people with the same values, personalities, and tendencies. But—and this is critically important—while you, as the CEO, may be the same person you were in the beginning, the organization's perception of you has changed. You are placed on a higher pedestal, and your actions and statements are more impactful because of your role. This elevated perception requires a higher level of awareness of yourself and the responsibilities that go along with the title and the weight they confer.

Most CEOs recognize the importance of what they say and do in formal settings like town halls and board meetings. They plan their communication and choose their words and tone carefully. Outside of those "official" meetings, however, most CEOs aren't as deliberate, mostly because they don't realize how powerful even the shortest comment or slightest action can be. In their head, they're still just one of the team. In that sense, the "shadow" cast by CEOs—whether intentional or not—has an outsized impact on how employees act, think, and feel.

While you, as the CEO, may be the same person you were in the beginning, the organization's perception of you has changed.

Howard coached a successful founder CEO who received feedback that he was creating a "wake" by changing policies and telling employees something different from the rest of the leadership team. He was completely caught off guard by the feedback and curious how his actions were creating issues. As the CEO dug deeper with Howard, it became clear the confusion and frustration could be traced back to one-on-one phone calls the CEO fielded while he was out of the office.

When he founded the company, the CEO was the only point of contact for all questions and issues. He openly committed to always being available to anyone. He valued his commitment so highly that even after the company grew significantly, he regularly took calls from employees when he was traveling, on-site with a client, out of the office on other company business, in the car, or in between meetings.

For the CEO, the primary importance of the calls was that he took them. Often, employees were calling with a question, and the CEO casually gave his thoughts or informally approved their requests. These calls were usually so short and informal that he didn't even remember many of them. He was shocked to learn that employees were taking what he said on these quick calls "as gospel" and immediately sharing what he had said to them with others. Sometimes, on these calls, the CEO was asked about things he wasn't involved in, and sometimes, he was asked if he would have any objection to a course of action. His thoughts and quick responses were occasionally inconsistent with the direction a department was moving in or the decisions that had already been communicated by others on his leadership team.

The CEO was open to the feedback, but he was genuinely surprised anyone gave his off-the-cuff comments so much weight. He didn't realize the influence he had on his employees. He prided himself on being one of them because he grew up in the industry and lived the same experiences they were living, but as the CEO, he'd been placed on a pedestal. What he perceived as informal conversations among peers had a significantly greater impact on his staff than he was aware of. His shadow was much larger than he appreciated. The experience was an "aha" moment that provided an opportunity to strengthen his leadership.

Strengthening leadership involves constantly elevating your self-awareness and understanding your impact. As the organization grows and embraces a leadership team approach, you can no longer operate "off the cuff." What worked at the Emerge stage no longer works in a larger and more complex environment.

EMBRACE MENTORING AND COACHING

It's lonely at the top. There's no one in the organization who has the same responsibilities, challenges, and stress you do, which means there's no one to talk to when you get stuck or are facing a complex decision.

While being the CEO may be lonely, you are not the only person who has faced these challenges. Finding an experienced mentor can be incredibly valuable. Someone who has experience successfully navigating the path you're on can save you substantial time and help you avoid pitfalls.

Many CEOs welcome having a mentor but aren't sure where to find one. Two of the greatest resources for industry insight and wisdom about scaling for founder CEOs are often their investors and their board. Unfortunately, CEOs sometimes resist seeking input and guidance from the board for fear such exploration will be misinterpreted as a sign of weakness. CEOs who are willing to seek and consider the advice of board members and investors with an open mind often find a path to becoming an even stronger leader.

To be clear, there is a fine line between seeking too much feedback from your board and too little. Both can be counterproductive. One CEO we know ended up out of a job when he answered, "I don't know," one too many times to board members' questions about serious challenges in the business. He relied too heavily on the board to help him find the answers. Ideally, the CEO will adeptly frame challenges for the board and engage board members in strategic discussions about the possible paths forward.

The challenges you face as a CEO can leave you stuck, feeling overwhelmed, and unclear about which direction or decision to choose. An experienced coach can help you find a clear path forward. If you ever feel like you're in your own way or have hit a wall you can't break through, we recommend seeking the guidance of a professional coach.

Coaching is valuable if there's a gap between where you are and where you want to be, and despite your best thinking, you are unable to bridge that gap on your own. An effective coach can help you reach your full professional and personal potential in a way that leverages your strengths and works best for you.

DISTRIBUTED LEADERSHIP

The CEO of a 100-person company found he was serving many masters. Whenever he had to make a decision, he consulted the group of senior leaders who founded the company (dubbed the Founder Class), he consulted a group of his top revenue producers, and he consulted the young, highly motivated rising stars. In total, he was talking to about 25 percent of the firm before he made a decision. Not only was this process inefficient; it also often left the CEO with whiplash from all the different opinions, yet still ultimately alone with his thoughts and the decision still weighing upon him.

He spent too much of his valuable time trying to involve

everyone and gain consensus. There wasn't enough time left over for the one thing that was the highest and best use of his time: the one thing no one else in the firm could do—focus on strategy. Our advice was to establish a leadership team and, in effect, *distribute* the job of leadership to more people. We worked with him to structure a team of mostly up-and-coming stars with a few long-tenured employees thrown in for balance and perspective. The group was eager to share the weight of leading the firm, and they took their new responsibilities seriously. They fully owned the success of the business.

The impact of this team-building move was monumental. It paved the way for new leadership to grow and established a strong pipeline for the future. It provided more career pathways for employees, which aided with retention. The leadership team took over the day-to-day responsibilities of running the business, and the CEO was finally elevated to his highest and best use—strategy. The business grew, and because the team was stable and strong, they were able to buy another company and successfully fold it into the mix. Recently, this same CEO reflected on this transformation and gave some sage advice: "The CEO has to be comfortable that the team is going to most likely execute differently than he did. You have to get over that. The truth is they're probably going to do it better, but it's going to be different. Your job is to empower, equip, and resource them and then to hold them accountable for the results. What does not work is micromanagement or saying, 'I would have done it this way.'"

One of the biggest challenges we see CEOs grapple with is their willingness to delegate real responsibility to others. No CEO can do it all.

Distributing leadership responsibilities makes the organization more resilient.

There's a reason you can't name a single person who made it famous as a one-man band, playing all the instruments at the same time. Distributing leadership responsibilities makes the organization more resilient, like a table with four legs or a diversified stock portfolio. It's able to weather unforeseen challenges more effectively and without the entire burden landing on a single individual.

Leading Others

The CEO's ability to lead others is a critical and evolving competency across the Four Stages of the Growth Gauntlet. We often use a musical analogy to illustrate how the role and competencies shift over time. At the outset of the business in the Emerge stage, the leader may be a soloist serving as the visionary and the only one leading the work. As the company grows, the soloist attracts additional musicians who play different instruments: product, sales, finance, and so on. All are playing largely equitable roles in the trio or quartet, except for the CEO, who is playing an instrument and leading the group, selecting the music, and scheduling rehearsals. At this stage, the CEO likely leads a critical function of the business, like product development.

As the company becomes more complex, the CEO hires someone else to play his instrument or, in this scenario, manage product development. The CEO then retires from playing an instrument and ascends to the leader of the band. Eventually, the band grows further in complexity; it might even become a full-scale orchestra. The bandleader's role elevates once again to conductor, which is a bandleader with a different set of skills. The conductor relies heavily on his section leaders, who work together to make the most beautiful music.

As an organization grows and becomes more complex, so does the role of the CEO.

In the beginning, the founder CEO focuses intensely on whatever tasks are required to get the business off the ground. Later, the CEO accomplishes the company's goals and objectives through other people. Leading and managing others is a skill set you have to learn, practice, and experience over time. As we said earlier, most founders start out with expertise in a product or service around which they build their company. Eventually, though, leadership and people management skills enable the CEO and the company to progress to the next stage of the Growth Gauntlet.

The Gauntlet is littered with founders who could not make the transition to people leaders. They were unwilling or unable to see they were preventing the company from growing and, ultimately, limiting value creation.

> **Leading and managing others is a skill set you have to learn, practice, and experience over time.**

Howard coached a founder CEO for several months. The CEO had created a healthcare information technology company, and he was very much an expert in both the product and the industry. When the company entered the Operationalize stage, he began to struggle to manage the employees, the leadership team, the board, the investors, *and* the product team. The board started to see some cracks and was concerned that he, like many CEOs before him, might not be able to make the leap from founder to people leader.

When he learned about the different stages in the Growth Gauntlet, he could see what the company needed from him, and he began to meet the challenges of this newly conceived role. He transitioned out of the day-to-day product manager into an executive role managing the strategy and the team. During coaching conversations and discussions with his board, he realized he had to build a strong leadership team to make the transition successfully—he had to get the right people in place and trust them to accomplish the company's goals. This CEO was great at product management, but once he let go, he found he was an even better CEO. He captured his growth trajectory when he told Howard, "I now think of my CEO role as being a chief leadership officer. My 'superpower' will be getting the right team, environment, guidance, incentives, and resources in place for great things to happen." Namaste! He saw the transition he needed to make, and he made it. And after a successful exit from that company, he was hired as the CEO of another high-growth company!

> **"I now think of my CEO role as being a chief leadership officer."**

STRENGTHENING TRUST

Leading others begins with building trust. Trust begets accountability and results. Pat Lencioni has written extensively on the importance of vulnerability-based trust and its role in high-performing teams. Vulnerability-based trust occurs when people feel they can speak openly and honestly without fear of reprisal, politics, or shame. They can admit to problems and share their strengths and gaps without worrying their honesty will be weaponized against them. This level of trust is completely contrary to the way most organizations operate. Most organizations deflect attention to others' mistakes and shortcomings instead of viewing themselves as a team of leaders who can help and complement one another's strengths and compensate for their weaknesses, which is why vulnerability-based trust does not develop overnight.

What does it look like to have a team that truly trusts one another? It means people feel comfortable putting all their cards on the table during conversations; they don't hold back information, suggestions, or concerns. They aren't afraid to examine their own performance to find the best path forward. And the group works toward solutions together and trusts their teammates will execute and meet the agreed-upon objectives.

People on highly trusting teams don't overpromise and underdeliver. They don't nonchalantly miss deadlines. They aren't chronically absent or late. They don't gossip and participate in office politics. They don't engage in backroom meetings where the rest of the team isn't present to defend themselves. They don't have a separate agenda from that of the rest of the team. If you are experiencing any of these behaviors, odds are you have a problem with trust and cohesion within your team.

To strengthen the effectiveness of your leadership team, you must first strengthen the trust level among the individuals on the team. Think about the team as the sum of the relationships team members have with one another. Those individual links make up the team's fabric and determine its strength. When even one link is strained, the team is weakened; that dysfunctional relationship dynamic can spill over and disrupt the whole group. Further, when you add a new member to a team that has been working together for a long time, you will have to allow some time and space for the new member to develop their trust links with the existing team members. It will take time and stewarding for the new team to regain the same level of trust and confidence and to operate at their highest performance potential.

> **Think about the team as the sum of the relationships team members have with one another.**

When asked, "How old is this team? How long has this team been working together?" people tend to respond according to when the original team was formed. The actual answer is very different. If the newest person on the team joined six months ago, then the team is only six months old, even if some people have been working together for ten years or more. As CEO, you need to view the team as a constantly evolving set of living, interactive relationships. Each time a new person is added, relationships need time to form and trust to grow.

What can you do to build a trusting leadership team? The first and most important steps are to make space for it and recognize trust must be nurtured intentionally and continuously.

Additionally, consider the following practices to further enhance your efforts:

- Establish a set meeting cadence for the team so they are together regularly and confronting problems and solutions together.

- Hold regular off-sites where team members can get to know one another outside of the office. Their relationships will be fortified, and they will become more comfortable and open as they learn more about one another while having fun and making some memories.

- Intentionally assign people who do not normally work together to tackle a strategic issue.

- Set up one-on-one lunches/meetings with each of the other team members within the first month to help new hires establish relationships and trust.

- Don't engage in or tolerate trust-damaging behaviors. If someone comes to you to vent about another person, direct them to the person in question, encourage direct dialogue, and offer ways to restore broken trust.

- Be willing to recognize when someone has irreparably broken the trust of the team and remove the person from the organization. A team is only as strong as its weakest link.

FOSTERING A CULTURE OF OPEN DISSENT

You'll know you've built a strong and trusting team when you have achieved a culture of open dissent, which is when the team feels comfortable enough with one another to disagree openly and come to the best solution for a problem. You absolutely do not want a leadership team that agrees with you 100 percent of the time. As the adage goes, "Iron sharpens iron." You want to surround yourself with the smartest people who have the best experience to take your organization to the next level. If you have established vulnerability-based trust, your team will engage in constructive debate, devise a path forward together, and accept the team's decision and support it. The goals are understanding and support, not consensus.

If your team is not accustomed to openly disagreeing, put them on the spot. It may take some time to develop this muscle. You can get them started by floating an idea and assigning half of the team to support the proposed solution and the other half to oppose it. In our own work, when one of us is preparing to present our findings to a client, we present a draft to our internal team and ask them "to shoot at it." These sessions are a lot of fun, and they force the person who drafted the material to defend their thesis. The exercise makes their presentation stronger and helps the author anticipate questions they may get from the client. We can honestly say we sleep much better the night before a big client presentation, knowing it has been thoroughly vetted by our team and revised accordingly.

PROVIDING CRITICAL FEEDBACK

Perhaps the toughest challenge of leading others is providing feedback. As we alluded to with open dissent, no one can grow without first understanding the behaviors they need to change. It's up to you, as a leader, to give constructive feedback and coach your employees to do their best work.

Kim Scott's 2017 book, *Radical Candor*, offers a great and simple approach to building strong working relationships with your direct reports. In sum, it requires you "give a damn" about the person and "be willing" to provide honest feedback to help the organization succeed and the person grow. As Scott says, one without the other leads to disastrous results. If you give critical feedback without caring, you're an asshole. If you care about the person but don't provide feedback, you're succumbing to "ruinous empathy," which means remaining silent while a person's performance deteriorates. The latter is a colossal waste of company time and resources and doesn't do anything for the person, either.

To strengthen your leadership team, sharpen your feedback skills. Feedback comes in several different forms. We coach CEOs to have regular one-on-one meetings with their direct reports so the feedback loop is in constant motion and there are no surprises.

The agenda might be as simple as the following:

1. What's working?
2. What's not working?

3. What are the barriers to your success, and how can I help to remove them?

These conversations go a long way to building trust and normalizing feedback for both the leader and the employee.

The most important part of giving feedback is approaching the conversation with the right mindset. Leaders generally approach feedback conversations from one of two mindsets:

1. Fixed: They view team members as unwilling or unable to do the work correctly (in which case, this is not a positive working relationship).

2. Growth: They assume positive intent, give the benefit of the doubt, and are curious why performance did not meet expectations.

If leaders approach feedback with a fixed mindset, they are not demonstrating they "give a damn" or "are willing" to help the person improve. If they approach feedback conversations with a growth mindset, the person is more likely to feel supported and be willing, and in many cases eager, to make changes.

It is important to understand your team members and their tendencies. A professional soccer coach we know studies films of his players' practices and games. Through this preparation, he arms himself intentionally with short, direct feedback, which he is able to deliver during games to quickly change a player's behavior. What we love about this is the highly emotional coach seen yelling from the sidelines is actually strategically prepared to share just the right feedback, at just the right moment, to change the game's outcome.

Be thoughtful, be constructive, and come prepared when you deliver feedback.

RECEIVING FEEDBACK

Perhaps even more important than being able to provide critical feedback is developing the ability to receive feedback without becoming defensive or dismissive. For most CEOs, it is rare to get feedback from anyone within your company—other than a comment or two on an anonymous engagement survey. It becomes necessary to ask for feedback from your leadership team and others within the organization.

There are two challenges with asking for feedback: First, most leaders are scared to receive honest and complete feedback, and second, when they do, it is often difficult to hear.

It's understandable that people are hesitant to give constructive feedback to the CEO, even if asked directly and assured that you really want their honest opinion. Most CEOs Howard has coached don't receive any meaningful feedback when they ask for it. Some interpret that to mean no one has any feedback. In reality, it's most often the result of a lack of trust. If you've never asked for feedback before, they may not think you're sincere or fear that, despite your assurances to the contrary, if they are honest, they will be in trouble. To get past this barrier, you have to be consistent in asking for feedback. More importantly, when they do provide feedback, you have to receive it well.

Asking for and receiving feedback should be seen, by default, as a listening event. Your role is to listen and, at the absolute most, ask clarifying questions to make sure you understand the feedback you are receiving.

The best response is often to simply say thank you and tell them how much you appreciate them sharing. If you get defensive, give reasons their perceptions are wrong, or seem dismissive, you will not only fail to learn, but you will also likely shut down any future feedback. Receiving feedback well will build trust, and your team will feel comfortable being candid with you.

MAKING DECISIONS

When Meg's husband, Scott, was just starting out as a young lawyer, a senior partner who was the attorney for a small municipality in Mississippi asked Scott to stand in for him at a city council meeting. Scott nervously responded, "I'm happy to do it, but I don't know anything." The elder attorney replied, "Don't worry. You will only get two kinds of questions: easy and hard. If it's an easy one, go ahead and answer it. If it's a hard one, just say, 'Councilman, that's a great question. I'm going to have to do some research on that and get back to you. If you will send me an email with exactly what you'd like me to research, I'll get my team on it this week.' They will appreciate that you complimented their intellect on the record and in front of their peers, and they'll never email you." Now, that's some wisdom!

The work of any organization can be distilled down to a collection of decisions individual employees make every day. And when they run into trouble, they escalate those decisions to their manager. Managers answer the easy questions, which means the hard questions are escalated up to the executive level.

In the early stages of the Growth Gauntlet, the CEO is involved in almost every decision, from the paint color of the office to product pricing and everything in between. As the organization grows, the CEO must rely on others to make decisions. The successful CEO is able to extract himself from the constant, day-to-day operational Q&A. This can be challenging because being needed can be personally fulfilling.

Two things can get CEOs into trouble with decision-making. The first is acting off the cuff without giving due consideration to a problem; the second is not acting fast enough, or living in a state of analysis paralysis. Another way to frame it is that some leaders take too much risk, and others don't take enough. Both paths are equally corrosive to trust and confidence.

One way to stay out of trouble is to develop the decision-making muscle of your leadership team to ensure tough challenges are met with the appropriate rigor and speed. Your first instinct, as the CEO, may be to figure out the solution on your own. Don't fall into that trap. You may own the final decision, but the path to good decision-making is to consult the experts on your team.

Define the problem and the timeline. Brainstorm with the team about what they will need to make a decision (data, information, research, etc.). Deploy the group to gather the information and set a time to come back together to share findings and potential solutions. In some cases, you won't need the whole team. Get the right people with the right information in the room and listen to their best thinking. Encourage open dissent. Assess the risks of each suggested solution. Understand you will likely have incomplete information, and you will have to act when you are only 80 percent ready.

Working through your team to make decisions pays tremendous dividends. The obvious one is you'll come to a better decision with the wisdom of more people around the table. The less obvious benefit is your team will value the experience and learn from it. By taking them on the decision-making journey with you, they will feel valued and respected. Even if they disagree with the direction you take, they will know you did your homework, their trust in you will be

> **Working through your team to make decisions pays tremendous dividends.**

enhanced, and they will support you as a leader. In addition, you will help them develop their decision-making skills. The stronger they are, the stronger the organization is.

ALLOW FOR FAILURE

The soccer coach we referenced earlier will readily tell you he's likely to be fired. He lives by the adage, "There are only two types of coaches: those who have been fired and those who are gonna be fired." In some ways, this mentality normalizes failure and frees the coaches from worrying about it.

The last thing an investor wants is a CEO who's more worried about his job than he is about advancing the organization's goals and initiatives. Such a person will be paralyzed when it comes to decision-making and unable to take risks. The soccer coach lost a game early in the season 7–0. Pretty crushing. His reaction? "I'd rather lose one game 7–0 than seven games 1–0." Truth. We're sure the club's owner would agree. And by the way, his team went on to win its division and play in the championship game.

Failure is only a good thing, though, if something can be learned from it. We're not talking about allowing for failures due to shoddy work. We're talking about taking calculated risks, where the team tried their best, but for one reason or another, it didn't work. When you lead others, it's your responsibility to empower your team to rewind the tape, review the film, extract the learning, and get back in the game.

Leading Strategy

CEOs lead both people and strategy. Organizations that stand still will fail, so leaders must be constantly evaluating and re-evaluating the directional strategy based on data and insights from inside and outside the organization. In Chapter 2, we discussed strategy and sharpening your organization's focus in detail. The key to strengthening leadership of strategy lies in staying one step ahead of everyone: the competition, the board, the team, and the customers. And to do so, leaders need to go both deep and wide.

GO DEEP

As a CEO, you have a unique perspective, and you are likely the only person who sees how all the parts of the business work together to produce results. The best CEOs deeply understand the intricate workings of their business. They know what levers to pull to create value. They constantly talk to people on the front lines to see what's working, what's changing, and what's not working, and they adjust accordingly. They review data and metrics to actively monitor the business, which gives them the ability to connect the dots across the organization and surface strategic initiatives to improve results.

Going deep provides endless insight to remediate problems, harvest efficiencies, innovate on products, and build out infrastructure. For example, an emerging SaaS business was focused on growing its top-line revenue. They were hitting their sales targets and bringing on new customers, but the company was leaking cash like a sieve. Data revealed the company had a churn problem; customers on month-to-month subscriptions were lured away by competitors after less than a year. The CEO took steps to build a "Save Ops" team to focus on retaining business. The Save Ops team focused exclusively on identifying and meeting proactively with the most at-risk clients. They were equipped with discounts and special incentives to retain these customers.

GO WIDE

Equally as important as going deep into strategy is going wide, and by that we mean going out into the world to see what else is happening in the market. Your company doesn't exist in a vacuum: You must regularly pick up your head and look around. Look at the competition and look at the horizon for big changes that could potentially disrupt your business. Staying current on trends, attending conferences, networking with peer companies, and listening to customer feedback are some of the best ways to stay ahead.

In the last year, we have sat in on no less than ten presentations from experts on AI and how it will change everything, just as cloud computing, the smartphone, and a whole list of other disruptive technologies did before it. Companies that are intentional about looking ahead and preparing for disruption—or that are intentionally creating their own—will have an advantage over those who don't. As one expert said to us, "Don't worry about AI taking your job; worry about the guy who bothered to understand AI taking your job."

Early in her career, Meg worked for an investment bank. Each year, she and her team interviewed hundreds of undergrads itching to be accepted into their two-year financial analyst program. As Meg and her team looked at the resumes, these Ivy League seniors were difficult to distinguish from one another. They all had GPAs hovering around a 4.0 and a slew of extracurricular activities to fill their time. As Meg and her team discussed an upcoming Super Saturday—a speed dating–style cattle call where dozens of candidates are interviewed in a round-robin format in a single morning—Meg expressed her angst over the task of selecting who would be the best fit. An older and wiser colleague told her, "The differentiator is intellectual curiosity. Find those who are curious about the world and use their discretionary time to learn. They will be the ones who ask the best questions, too." He was absolutely right, and she has found his insight to be true throughout the course of her career.

Howard has had the same experience with his coaching engagements. He sees the greatest leadership growth and effectiveness in CEOs who are curious about what they don't know, humble enough to hear it, and committed enough to do something about it. Curious people are never satisfied. There is always something more to discover, more to the story, more than meets the eye. They are always learning. They tend to have interesting hobbies. They work for the value the experience brings, and the compensation comes second.

As a CEO, cultivating a sense of curiosity is critical. Curiosity can be deep and wide, too. For example, if you're the CEO of a company in the healthcare space, you may spend a good part of your discretionary time staying current in the healthcare industry. But being curious about things outside your specific industry is equally important. What you learn about other topics—industries, technologies, cultures, religions, politics, and geographies—helps you think critically and connect important dots for your strategy and your team. It may even make you a great cocktail party guest, which helps build your network!

Meg was talking to a friend who is an airline pilot, and she asked him about the interview process to become a pilot. He told her the most important thing, again, was intellectual curiosity. Why? "Because," he replied, "you're looking for someone you'd want to spend a lot of time with in the cockpit."

The CEO we referenced earlier, who built out his leadership team, now has the time to focus on his passion and strength: strategy.

He has carved out white space on his calendar to think, read, and get smart on topics that will impact the business down the road. He has put together a study group composed of other curious people across the organization. They meet regularly and trade articles and podcast suggestions with one another, all with the simple goal of "getting smarter" on the latest technology advances. It's too early to tell what will come from this effort, but it's already paying dividends through employee engagement and learning. And the board has renewed trust and confidence in him because they see he is focused on the long-term success of the business. His initiatives to strengthen his own leadership skills, the skills of those around him, and to lead the organization's strategy are evident in his curiosity, his relationships, and the bottom line.

Strengthening Leadership across the Four Stages of the Growth Gauntlet

They say it's "lonely at the top" for a reason. It's as if you're the only person standing at the top of the mountain, with a view of your troops coming up behind you, and a view up ahead of the advancing enemy forces. You've got to lead yourself, lead your troops, and formulate the battle plan. As if that's not enough, the battles get more and more complex with larger stakes during each stage of the Growth Gauntlet.

It's the rare entrepreneur who can lead a business through all Four Stages of the Growth Gauntlet. In fact, if you were to draft a job description for the CEO at each of the four stages, those job descriptions would be completely different. The necessary skills and experience for a CEO at each of the stages bear little resemblance to one another.

Evolution of the CEO Role

Emerge CEO	Operationalize CEO	Thrive CEO	Explore & Expand CEO
Entrepreneurial	Process-driven	Financially savvy	Completely out of day-to-day management
Passionate and inspirational	Working toward standardization	Leader of teams and strategy	Face of the company
Immersed in the work of proving concept	Builder of teams	Developer of talent	Exceptional developer of talent
Leads a critical function in addition to being CEO	Manager of day-to-day operations	Great communicator	Exceptional communicator

In the Emerge stage, an entrepreneur creates a vision and inspires people to join him in making it a reality. This stage requires someone who is both a visionary and a builder. Successful founder CEOs tend to be creative, charismatic, and driven to prove their ideas will succeed, and they have a high tolerance for risk.

By contrast, the Operationalize stage leader is focused, disciplined, and capable of building processes and accountability. The successful CEO in this stage is one who is a systems thinker and who can focus the organization on a few very specific priorities. The operational leader seeks to de-risk the organization by creating structures to ensure the products and services are produced consistently and efficiently. During the Operationalize stage, the founder CEO from the Emerge stage, with his constant barrage of new ideas and desire to chase shiny objects, is counterproductive to the strategy (often becoming what we call the "chief distraction officer"). For the Operational leader to be effective, she will have to control innovation, so it does not overwhelm or distract the organization from its focus.

In the Thrive stage, there is a shift in focus from internal operations to external considerations. The Thrive stage CEO must be concerned with building a sustainable customer base and growing revenue. By the time the organization is in the Thrive stage, it will likely have outside investors and a board. The CEO's skill set must include the ability to woo enterprise clients, manage both the investors and the board, and look for strategic opportunities for inorganic growth (M&A), among other things. Also, at this stage, the management team is larger and more experienced; they require a leader who is a mature manager and developer of people, who can lead without being in the weeds of the day-to-day operations, and who can build a team and hold them accountable.

And finally, the Explore and Expand stage needs a leader who is skilled in a little bit of everything: a CEO with a passion for innovation, an appreciation for execution, and a strategic mind for enterprise-level partnerships. Plus, a leader at this stage should possess the ability to manage multiple constituents: employees, shareholders, investors, boards, and customers.

The Explore and Expand CEO likely sits atop a large, complex organization. Like a Thrive stage leader, this leader must be skilled at building an experienced leadership team and holding them accountable for results. This leader is a strong developer of talent and is constantly strengthening the leadership team to ensure it is staffed to execute the strategy at hand. She is a world-class communicator able to connect with frontline employees about the importance of their work and shareholders about value creation and strategy. The Explore and Expand leader stands on the bow of the ship, with an eye on the horizon, navigating the vessel that requires a large and diverse crew with many special skills to operate.

Meg managed the two-year investment banking analyst program for Credit Suisse in the 1990s. She noticed a disconnect between the skills they were looking for in an analyst and those that would make a successful senior banker someday. The most important skills for the young analyst were quantitative. The company sought the undergraduates with the highest GPAs and SAT scores in math. But these analysts rarely lasted longer than two years unless they had another skill: communications. Banking is ultimately a relationship business. To move up in the organization requires people expertise. The same is true for CEOs. Most CEOs start out in finance, engineering, or product. They have highly technical skills. As you move up in the organization, two skills eclipse those early ones: communication and talent development. Successful CEOs are those who are adept at navigating, inspiring, mobilizing, and coaching people. CEOs are in the relationship business.

The point is leadership looks different at each stage of the Growth Gauntlet and requires a new CEO job description. That description should be written for the specific challenges the organization will face during that stage and detail the new set of skills and experiences needed to be successful. Very rarely will a founder CEO stay at the helm through all Four Stages of the Growth Gauntlet, and, we would argue, never without a strong team of leaders around her and the self-awareness and self-discipline to let the team lead from the front.

Leadership looks different at each stage of the Growth Gauntlet and requires a new CEO job description.

We believe if entrepreneurs and investors have the knowledge to understand and openly discuss the different stages of the Growth Gauntlet and the different skills needed in each stage on the front end of their growth journey, they can eliminate the surprises and friction that often lead to unnecessary value-destroying drama.

Leveling Up: The Strategic Edge

Critical Questions for the CEO to Ask Herself/Himself

1. Do I have the skills and mindset needed for the stage of growth we are in?

2. What am I doing for my own growth and development and to strengthen my own self-awareness as a leader?

3. What are my blind spots and weaknesses, and what kind of person is important for me to have on my team to complement my strengths and gaps?

4. Are there any weak trust links on my leadership team? If so, how can I help to strengthen those?

5. What am I doing to elevate my leadership to the next stage, from individual musician to conductor?

Critical Questions for the CEO to Ask the Leadership Team

1. Are we leading as standard-bearers for the culture? Why or why not? How can we improve?

2. My intention is to empower this leadership team. Are there any ways I am unintentionally undermining you?

3. Do we have a culture of open dissent? Why or why not? How can we foster it?

4. Do you believe that I am spending time on only the things that are the highest value and best use for me to do? If not, why not?

5. Do you feel like you, as a part of my leadership team, are getting the right amount and level of feedback from me?

6. Is our team effective at making decisions? How can we improve?

Critical Questions for the Board to Ask

1. Do we have the right CEO for the stage of growth we are in?

2. Is leadership appropriately distributed across a strong leadership team or too closely held by the CEO?

3. Does the CEO make decisions too quickly without enough consideration, or not quickly enough with too much analysis?

4. Is our CEO appropriately focused on long-term strategy?

5. Does a culture of open dissent exist among board members such that when a crisis occurs, board members have established trust and can effectively work together to manage the issue?

Milestones and Initiatives

- Host regular off-sites to strengthen trust among leadership team members.

- Institute regular one-on-ones with direct reports to provide and receive feedback.

- Carve out white space to spend time thinking, learning, networking, and growing in your ability to lead strategy.

Strengthen Leadership Quick Reference

Stages of Growth			
Emerge Informal, Ad Hoc, Undefined, Reactive	**Operationalize** Defined, Data-Informed, Focused, Proactive	**Thrive** Accountable, Data-Driven, Predictable	**Explore & Expand** Strategic, Agile, Innovative, Opportunistic
Organization is founder-led. Leaders wear many hats. Roles are not explicitly defined.	CEO is player/coach with heavy operational responsibilities. Leadership team is loose confederation of functional leaders. Key experienced hires are needed to round out team.	Highly competent, cohesive, aligned leadership team is in place. Each leadership team member owns a key strategy or function critical to success. CEO's time increasingly externally focused on growth.	CEO is mostly focused on strategic opportunities. Leadership team has full ownership of day-to-day operations and wears both functional and strategic hats.

What is it?

- Lead Yourself
- Lead Others
- Lead Strategy

What's the value?

Leadership sets the course, inspires the troops, and holds each other accountable. The hallmark of a strong leadership team is vulnerability-based trust that allows for open dissent to find the best solutions.

CHAPTER 5

Elevate Talent

"People are not your most important asset. The right people are."
—Jim Collins

WHEN MEG WAS AT GOOGLE in the early 2000s, the company fell into the trap of hiring the *best* people. Because Google was such a popular place to work, it was able to set high benchmarks (GPAs, test scores, Ivy League schools, etc.) and accept only those who cleared the artificially high hurdles. To be clear, you did not need an Ivy League degree to work at Google, but the application pool was filled with these high achievers, including newly minted graduates from Stanford, which was just down the street. Google was out to hire the best and the brightest, and conventional wisdom dictated that those were Stanford grads. At a minimum, screening for college pedigree offered the overwhelmed recruiters an easy way to cull the stack of resumes. So, Google pressed on with this method until they learned the lesson the hard way.

Many people wanted a job—any job—at Google's Mountain View campus. The word on the street was that if you wanted a job at Google, apply for a receptionist position, then wait six months, and you'd get pulled into product development or sales. And that's how it came to be that Google had a preponderance of overqualified, bright-eyed, Stanford-educated receptionists who did not stay receptionists for very long.

The problem was Google really did need receptionists, ideally, people who wanted to be receptionists and were content—even enthusiastic—about the role and who wanted to stay in it for longer than six months. You could argue that Google was hiring the cream of the crop. In reality, they were missing the mark in a huge way.

You can't outperform your people.

It's hard to overstate the value of talent in the knowledge economy. We've seen a remarkable shift in the way people work and what kinds of work our economy values. As we mentioned earlier, when we started our careers, people were called "employees." Now, employees are called "talent," and this new moniker is emblematic of the importance of people and their outsized impact on driving results, especially in high-growth businesses.

Companies are buzzing with "talent management" processes, "talent recruitment" initiatives, and "talent development" programs. Highly skilled jobs require companies to invest time and energy training employees because, in reality, you can't outperform your people.

There is an old cartoon that shows two managers talking. One says, "What if we train our people and they leave?" and the other says, "What if we don't and they stay?" This dichotomy accurately represents the challenges inherent in elevating talent, which is essentially an exercise in value creation through your people.

Three Rules to Live By

Elevating talent requires three actions:

1. Hire better talent

2. Develop the talent you have

3. Liberate poor performers

HIRE BETTER TALENT

Larry Page got it right when he put hiring strong talent at the top of his strategic priorities. Talent continues to be one of Google's key competitive advantages. But hiring better talent is not as easy as it sounds. It's not necessarily about hiring the talent with the most impressive credentials.

> **The key to hiring better talent is to hire slowly.**

It's far more nuanced. It's about hiring the best people for the role, for your Stage of Growth, and for your culture.

The key to hiring better talent is to hire slowly. Doing the hard work on the front end, to really dig into the scope of responsibility, the skill sets, qualifications, and attitudes you're hiring for will save a lot of heartache and headache on the back end. As one former CEO likes to say, "Hire hard, manage easy." Before you post a job opening or interview a single candidate, ensure you have done your own thorough internal due diligence.

Create an Internal Pre-Hire Checklist

1. Know thyself. Make sure the organization understands its culture and how to identify those who will thrive within it. Develop interview questions for each of your core values and train your staff on how to assess cultural fit.

2. Align around the role. If you are the hiring manager, enlist the help of key stakeholders who will work with this person to tell you what they need. Get everyone on the same page about the role and what success looks like before the interviews. There's nothing worse than interviewers giving conflicting descriptions of the role to candidates! Alignment ensures consistency across interviewers in the criteria used to evaluate candidates.

3. Focus on the future, not the past. Each time you go to market, you have an opportunity to level up. Has the strategy evolved since the last person was hired? What skills are necessary now and in the future to achieve the strategy? Can this role fill an existing skills gap on the team? Does the role need to be split or specialized—for example, did the previous person in the position do the work of two, or even three, people?

4. Always interview multiple candidates so you have an opportunity to compare and contrast and come to a better decision. (You'd be surprised how often leaders hire and promote people without interviewing multiple candidates.) For consistency, a best practice is to have the same interviewers meet all the candidates so they are working from the same data set.

5. Check references. Costly hiring mistakes can be easily avoided with a simple phone call. Use every resource available to vet

your candidates, beginning with their previous employers and including people who have managed them and those whom they have managed.

If your team is looking to adopt a wholesale hiring process, we recommend Geoff Smart and Randy Street's book *Who: The A Method for Hiring*. It lays out a great system for operationalizing your hiring practices and developing the organizational competency of elevating talent. More on their methods later in this chapter.

DEVELOP THE TALENT YOU HAVE

A bird in hand is worth two in the bush. If you have people who have passed the culture hurdle, who have bought into your vision, and who have growth potential, then, by all means, invest in them. Help them develop the skills and knowledge to contribute even more value to the organization.

Training and development come in many forms:

- Operational training (what I need to know to perform my job, e.g., software, safety, processes, operations)
- Employee development (how I can do my job better by optimizing my skills and strengths)
- Leadership training (how to lead myself and others)
- Mentoring/coaching (learning from those ahead of me)
- Professional certifications (external courses that contribute to building my skill set)

Each of these training modalities has an important role to play in helping employees up their game. Certainly, the more knowledge and experience an employee has, the more value they can add.

Another key benefit of investing in training and development is retention. Employees who are actively learning and who feel like the company is investing in them are more likely to stick around longer, which increases your ROI on the training investment and contributes to organizational stability.

LIBERATE POOR PERFORMERS

In the 1990s, when Meg was running the two-year investment banking analyst program, no one ever got fired. There were certainly poor performers, but by the time managers identified them, there were only a few months left on the clock, so it wasn't worth the hassle. One time, there was a smart, talented recent graduate of a pedigreed school who was reportedly spending all his time in the corporate gym. It was clear this guy needed to go, and the boss decided Meg was the one who had to do it.

She had never terminated anyone before and was so nervous about it she didn't sleep for a week. All she could think about was that she was destroying his promising career. It was agony. Finally, the day came; she delivered the message, and he was gone.

A few months later, she was on a plane from New York to San Francisco for work, indulging in her favorite magazine, *Vanity Fair*. Flipping through the ads, something—or someone—caught her eye. The analyst she fired was the male model in a six-page spread for a big fashion house. She could not believe it. Getting fired was the best thing to ever happen to him!

Since then, she's reflected on this story and the many subsequent people in her career she's had to terminate, lay off, or counsel out. Now, she sincerely believes everyone deserves to find a place they can thrive, where they can add value and be valued. And when people are not positioned to thrive—for any number of reasons—it's profoundly important to set them free. We've never heard anyone say they regretted terminating an employee; we've only heard them lament about how long it took to make the decision.

Poor performers fall into two buckets: coachable and not coachable. Those who are coachable may lack the skills or experience to execute on a certain task, but can, with training or mentorship, get there. Those who repeatedly violate the culture and the general rules of work are not coachable. For example, a toxic employee might meet all of her goals but leave a trail of metaphorical dead bodies: a team feeling demoralized and unproductive.

> **Everyone deserves to find a place where they can thrive.**

Poor performers are a drag on the entire organization. Their inability to pull their weight and/or their negative behaviors put extra pressure on the top performers, creating resentment and decreased morale. People tend to be enormously relieved when a problem person on their team has been terminated, and, in many cases, productivity improves, so don't hang on to the bad apples.

Howard was facilitating a leadership team retreat, and one employee's name came up several times in the context of things that weren't getting done the way they needed to be. Each leader expressed frustration, but there was a resigned tone. When Howard asked the team to envision a scenario where the employee won the lottery and resigned, there was an immediate and visible reduction in the angst and stress. The follow-up question was "If, a month later, he decided he wanted to come back, would you rehire him?" They struggled to say it at first, but they all concluded they would not rehire him. Once they said it out loud, they started thinking about what that role could be and how they would fill it. At the end of their brainstorming session, they decided they needed to let him go.

There's an old story about the man who took his dog to the vet. The vet told the man his dog had cancer in his tail, and it needed to be removed. The man hated the thought of his dog losing his tail, so instead of cutting off the whole tail at once, he cut it off one inch at a time! Poor dog. No one likes firing people, and we go to great lengths to avoid it. We all want to spare people the awkward moment, but letting such a big decision languish is like cutting off the tail an inch at a time: painful, unnecessary, and simply delaying the inevitable.

An additional consideration is you can liberate a poor performer from a position but not from the entire organization. Some high performers get hired or promoted into roles that aren't a good fit for their strengths or the role evolves away from their strengths. The mismatch creates friction and poor performance, but there may be other positions where an employee could add value. It's always wise to take a strategic look at the entire organization and at least consider whether a move is valuable. This is not the same as moving someone around because you don't like confrontation or don't want to fire them out of a sense of loyalty or friendship, which is a no-no.

Performance Management: It's a Tool, Not a Weapon

Performance management has changed dramatically in the last 20 years. The annual look-back has been deemed ineffective, out of date, and insufficient to keep up with talent progress or challenges in real time. These days, performance management is an active tool for driving results. To drive results through your people, your performance review process should include frequent feedback, forward-looking professional goals, and career development that reinforces your culture.

In the Emerge stage of a company's life, there is very little performance management. Positive performance at this stage is the result of a team built on raw loyalty to the founder and his or her idea. It's trench warfare, and everyone is working with an intense survival mentality. And frankly, a warm body is better than nobody at all. As the company grows, becomes less founder-centric, and more employees are hired to perform specific tasks, the need for accountability and oversight emerges. Establishing a company-wide performance management system is critical.

Let us put your mind at rest: If you are in the Operational or Thrive stage, you don't need to spend $50,000 on a performance management system. In fact, one of the worst things you can do is to adopt a model used by a 50,000-person company and apply it to a 200-person company. That would be like using a missile to kill a mosquito; the process will collapse under its own weight.

There is no one-size-fits-all model. The important thing is to develop a process, structure, and cadence for actively managing performance and to ensure it happens regularly. At the heart of performance management is a conversation between a manager and an employee in which both parties provide feedback to the other on what's working and what's not. Any process or practice needs to facilitate that conversation.

Basics of a Performance Management Process

1. Set clear expectations.
2. Check in regularly to see how things are going.
3. Provide specific and actionable feedback.
4. Invite specific and actionable feedback and listen.

5. Provide opportunities for professional growth and skills development.

6. Simplify what's working and what's not.

7. Be curious and nonjudgmental.

8. Don't lose sight of the employee's humanity.

9. Lather. Rinse. Repeat.

It's that simple! No fancy system is required. Howard is a fan of the Situation-Behavior-Impact (SBI) tool, which is a simple and direct process to facilitate conversations between a manager and an employee. Discuss the *situation* that occurred. What happened? Where and when did it happen? And what was the specific *behavior* in question? What was the *impact* of that behavior on the team or organization? Also, Kim Scott's best-selling book *Radical Candor*, described as a cultural touchstone, presents a lot of useful information for business leaders at companies both large and small to communicate feedback and facilitate difficult conversations.

SAMPLE: ANNUAL PERFORMANCE REVIEW SCHEDULE

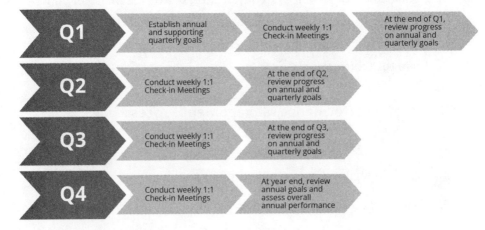

Q1 — Establish annual and supporting quarterly goals — Conduct weekly 1:1 Check-in Meetings — At the end of Q1, review progress on annual and quarterly goals

Q2 — Conduct weekly 1:1 Check-in Meetings — At the end of Q2, review progress on annual and quarterly goals

Q3 — Conduct weekly 1:1 Check-in Meetings — At the end of Q3, review progress on annual and quarterly goals

Q4 — Conduct weekly 1:1 Check-in Meetings — At year end, review annual goals and assess overall annual performance

The scorecards we referenced earlier, from the book *Who: The A Method for Hiring*, are also an effective performance management tool. A scorecard sets expectations at the beginning of employment and is updated annually to adjust for new goals and expectations. Smart and Street's scorecard has four sections: Mission, Key Outcomes, Role-Based Competencies, and Cultural Competencies.

The Mission addresses the question of why the role exists. It helps to tie the role to the overall vision and goals of the company so that the employee understands the value of their role for the success of the business. For example, the mission for a scorecard related to a sales position might describe the role's focus on revenue generation, or a customer support role's scorecard might reference maintaining high customer satisfaction, a core value of the company.

The Key Outcomes section lists the three to five most important objectives for the role. These should be quantifiable goals or milestones such that a manager and employee can easily agree on whether the outcome was achieved or not. Unlike a job description, where we tend to throw in every possible responsibility a person might conceivably have, the scorecard's key outcomes are meant to be a set of priorities to help focus the employee on what is most important for the business to succeed. The key outcomes should be listed in order of priority and will likely change year over year.

The Role-Based Competencies list the important skills an employee must have to be successful in the role. For example, the CFO's scorecard would list financial skills, the CTO's scorecard would list technical skills, and the CEO's scorecard would list both of those plus communication skills and more. These five to eight competencies are meant to be the most important skills a person in this role must have.

And finally, last but certainly not least, the Cultural Competencies describe how a company expects the employee to behave in accordance with their culture and core values. Translate your core values into core competencies and use those competencies for all employees' scorecards. This section of the scorecard is critically important because it helps managers address challenging behavioral issues. It's very straightforward to coach and, ultimately, terminate someone who does not meet their key outcomes. More challenging and subjective is coaching or disciplining people for behaving in culturally inappropriate ways. By adding these competencies to the scorecard, you'll be sure to set clear cultural expectations and periodically discuss any issues related to an employee's behavior.

USING THE SCORECARD FOR PERFORMANCE MANAGEMENT

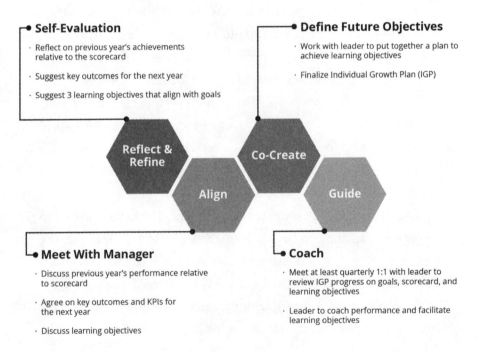

Self-Evaluation

· Reflect on previous year's achievements relative to the scorecard

· Suggest key outcomes for the next year

· Suggest 3 learning objectives that align with goals

Define Future Objectives

· Work with leader to put together a plan to achieve learning objectives

· Finalize Individual Growth Plan (IGP)

Reflect & Refine

Align

Co-Create

Guide

Meet With Manager

· Discuss previous year's performance relative to scorecard

· Agree on key outcomes and KPIs for the next year

· Discuss learning objectives

Coach

· Meet at least quarterly 1:1 with leader to review IGP progress on goals, scorecard, and learning objectives

· Leader to coach performance and facilitate learning objectives

It's best to establish scorecards collaboratively with employees. Doing so will ensure alignment between manager and employee on expectations and an employee's buy-in on their goals. The previous graphic references the process steps for managers to establish scorecards collaboratively with their employees.

Once the scorecard is built and both parties have agreed to it, a manager and an employee can use it as the basis for quarterly check-in conversations to discuss how things are going:

- What has been accomplished?
- Have the priorities changed?
- What roadblocks need to be removed?
- Is the employee in danger of not meeting goals?
- What can the manager do to course correct?

Both the manager and the employee receive important feedback in this conversation. The manager gets a better understanding of what is (or is not) being accomplished, which helps inform their oversight. And the employee gets important feedback on what they are doing well and what needs improvement. After the conversation, the employee can summarize the major points in a short memo to be signed by both parties. The memo plus the scorecard provides a blueprint for the next quarter's conversation.

It's important to review the scorecard quarterly versus annually for a couple of reasons. First, quarterly meetings offer a more frequent opportunity for managers to help course correct an employee who is not performing well. Secondly, studies have shown that annual feedback suffers a "recency effect," meaning the employee is actually

Sample Employee Scorecard

Role:		Software Engineer (Backend Developer)
Mission:		Software Engineers develop and maintain Acme's products: a suite of revenue maximizing software solutions. SWEs translate design specifications provided by Solutions Architects and Product Owners into sustainable, usable software using good practices and the principles of the Agile method.

Key Outcomes		
1.		Successfully launch <Product Name/Release> by <date>.
		Successfully complete coding assignments as defined by the Engineering Leadership team and Product Owners on time and meeting high standards for code quality including developing clear, well-documented, peer-reviewed, high-quality code as measured by:
		Sprint contribution as measured by 75% average contribution
		95% or greater on Committed vs. Completed Story Points
		Customer Satisfaction Survey scores of 4.5 or greater
		No more than 10% of completed tasks rejected by QA
		Resolve 100% of incidents without impacting success of overall sprint
2.		Collaboration and best practices
		Participate in peer code reviews related to technical skill set
		Prioritize all sprint-related work over non-sprint-related work
		Willingly share information with team members daily, regarding progress, expertise
		Consistently document work so that others can follow
3.		Grow as a developer
		Stay current on coding languages
		Learn new relevant coding skills, technologies
		Train others
		<personalize professional development opportunities>

Selected Competencies	
Role-Based Competencies (5-8)	
	Ability to write software in: .Net, C#, MySQL, PostgreSQL, MS SQL, PowerShell, Python, PHP, Visual Studio
	Strong intellectual curiosity, ability to ask good questions, and learn new technologies
	Ability to listen to stakeholders, take feedback, and course correct
	Ability to analyze and solve complex problems
Cultural Competencies (5-8)	
	Personal accountability
	Clear and concise communication
	Team player who collaborates well with and appreciates others
	Positive attitude and ability to enjoy the work

only given feedback on the previous three months or what constitutes recent memory for the reviewer. Employees lose the opportunity for positive and negative feedback for three quarters of the year. And, finally, employees want feedback and to know how they are doing. Checking in on performance quarterly is an effective tool for managing employees and the business.

Middle Managers: A Critical Layer of Leadership

One key challenge high-growth companies face is building out the first layer of middle managers. If you are short on resources and have to pick one cohort to invest in, put your time and money into building strong middle management, a critical layer of leadership when your company grows beyond 50 employees. The benefits of a strong management bench include improved communication, culture, retention, and leadership continuity.

Invariably, the process of building the middle management team begins with promoting a star individual contributor into a people manager role. It usually happens like this: "Hey, Jack is our best fill-in-the-blank, so he should manage the team!" The skill set necessary for people management is entirely separate and apart from an employee's functional skill set. So, it's critical to recognize people management requires certain competencies and intentional development. For example, an excellent software engineer will not necessarily make for an excellent software engineering manager. Upper management often makes the mistake of assuming someone will be an excellent manager simply because they are an excellent individual contributor, which is very rarely the case.

A manager is responsible for a team of people. The number of people a manager is responsible for is referred to as the "span of control," and it varies depending on the complexity, type, size, and culture of the company. Span-of-control conversations tend to emerge in the Operationalize stage of the Growth Gauntlet when the team grows beyond the two-pizza rule. Jeff Bezos famously determined that when two pizzas are no longer enough for a team to share, it's time to divide the cell and become two teams.[15] The ideal team size is seven to nine people, which is about two slices each. A manager can comfortably lead and regularly meet with that number of people. And a team of that size can discuss a topic or work through a problem in a way that all voices are heard. When a team grows beyond nine people, getting work accomplished together becomes more challenging. And managers will have a harder time staying on top of regular one-on-one meetings to ensure team members' goals, development, and projects are adequately supervised.

As effective as the two-pizza rule can be, there are certain circumstances when it is not an appropriate barometer, such as when a large number of people are essentially performing the same function and do not require as much oversight. For example, a call center manager can be responsible for dozens of employees. Their task set is relatively narrow and well-defined; it does not vary dramatically from one person to the next, the volume of work is fairly consistent, and the results are measured by individual performance. In contrast, a marketing team may consist of writers, graphic designers, web developers, and branding experts. Each of these roles requires differing, specialized skill sets all working to complete projects. Managing a specialized, collaborative team requires more oversight, and completing the project requires the team to be in constant communication.

A manager's core responsibility is to set the priorities for their team and ensure those priorities are aligned with the overall business strategy. They must also ensure those goals are met and in a way that is consistent with the company's culture. Most employees, especially in larger companies, only experience the company through their experience with their primary team and team leader. The CEO and Executive Leadership Team may be too far removed to impact most employees' lives directly. That's why team leaders, or managers, are the most important people in the organization. They are the direct conduits from executive leadership to the individual employees. The manager is a key source of information for his or her employees, a key gatekeeper for opportunities, and a cultural role model.

Google's People Operations team under Laszlo Bock studied their employee population and proved the old adage true: People don't quit companies; they quit managers. In his 2015 book, *Work Rules! Insights from Inside Google That Will Transform How You Live and Lead*, Laszlo laid out the list of key competencies or behaviors that were identified among the most successful people managers at Google:

1. Is a good coach

2. Empowers team and does not micromanage

3. Creates an inclusive team environment, showing concern for others' success and well-being

4. Is productive and results oriented

5. Is a good communicator, listens and shares information

6. Supports career development and discusses performance

7. Has a clear vision/strategy for the team

8. Has key technical skills to help advise the team

9. Collaborates across the company

10. Is a strong decision-maker

These skills are not specific to big tech or software engineering managers. Regardless of your industry, these are the competencies to look for in your individual contributors before promoting them to middle managers. But putting the right people in a people manager role is only half the battle.

The next step is training them on *the practice of people management*. What do we mean by management practices? Every company is unique, but most companies have certain tasks and decisions that managers are responsible for, such as recruitment, hiring, training, development, and performance management. People managers need to know what is expected of them in each of these critical functions.

For example, a data center company wanted to codify its management practices so that it could ensure consistency across the company. The Executive Leadership Team worked together in a retreat setting to agree upon a set of best practices and core competencies for managers. The session and the agreed-upon framework provided a blueprint for HR, so they, in turn, were able to design and develop manager training. Here's what they came up with:

Management Practices

1. Weekly team meeting

2. Quarterly scorecard review with each direct report

3. Weekly one-on-one meetings with each direct report

4. Practice principles of meeting hygiene

5. Cascade communication

6. Manage according to established HR/legal/financial guidelines/guardrails

7. Be a cultural role model

And, remember, each of these activities takes time. Those who may have been promoted to people manager from an individual contributor role will need to adjust their productivity accordingly. The task of managing people often takes 25–50 percent of a person's time, depending on the number of direct reports they have. We have listed some of the many tasks managers take on when managing a team of people in the following chart.

Elevating Talent

Hiring	Developing	Managing
Organizational planning	Culture training	Planning and running team meetings
Sourcing/Networking	Vocational training	Communicating strategy to the team
Interviewing	Hold 1:1 meetings	Culture building activities
Onboarding	Setting developmental goals	Removing roadblocks
	Looking for development opportunities	
	Providing performance feedback	

It's important to note here that not everyone wants to manage and/or has the skills to manage and that's okay. Meg had a conversation with a frustrated CEO recently. He has an employee who performs exceptionally well and is highly valued for his analytical skill set. The challenge is that to be promoted to the next level requires this employee to develop business (to sell). Despite all of his coaching, the CEO reports that this person is not rising to the business development challenge.

Here's the thing: A tiger cannot change his stripes. This person may not ever excel at sales but will still be tremendously valuable to the organization for his natural abilities with numbers. Meg coached the CEO to have a conversation with the employee and ask him what he wants to do in the future. Does he want to move up in the ranks and take on the dreaded sales role? If so, they can have an honest conversation on how to do that. If not, they can have an honest conversation about his future with the company. The company may choose to keep him as a valued individual contributor or may decide to help him find a similar role elsewhere.

Google realized this early with its engineers and created dual career paths, one for software engineering managers and another for software engineers as individual contributors. Both are highly valued at Google, but one requires a managerial skill set in addition to the engineering skill set.

Build a Self-Replicating Talent Machine

Laszlo Bock discusses the concept of a self-replicating talent machine (SRTM) in his book *Work Rules!* An SRTM is an organization that has developed the skills, processes, and programs to bring people into the organization and quickly train them to the level of productivity necessary to meet the demands of the business. Companies that have built this organizational competency are far better able to weather the inevitable peaks and troughs that are part and parcel of the Growth Gauntlet.

CASE IN POINT: TRAINING IS EVERYONE'S JOB

A digital media company received a sizable investment from a private equity firm, and the team was excited about the prospect of explosive growth. New sales resources turned on the revenue faucet, and the company was quickly in over its head. This young team was full of bright, hardworking, and talented people who were not afraid to work long hours and come in on the weekends if needed. The problem was no one had the capacity to train and mentor new employees to get them to the necessary level of productivity quickly. They were caught in a common bind; they could either service their clients (for which they got paid) or train new hires (for which they did not get paid). The organization was not scalable. Elevating talent was the limiting factor to growth.

To solve the problem, the company reacted predictably. Having just received a capital infusion, they were flush with cash, so they hired *even more* people and chose to blame the previous hires for their inability to get to productivity on their own. That scenario, of course, exacerbated the problem in two ways. First, the current employees lacked the capacity to interview candidates, so they were overly reliant on recruiters to screen and interview candidates, which led to weak hiring decisions and turnover. Second, they had more people to train and no one to train them.

The company's next move was also predictable. They hired a director of training to build—or, rather, outsource—training altogether. This initiative failed (as it usually does) because you cannot bring in someone from the outside to train your new hires. Your people are the experts on their work, your clients, your internal processes, and your intellectual property. They have to replicate themselves. Everyone's job description must include training.

Ultimately, we helped them come around to a sustainable and

scalable solution: build a training culture, empower key people with the capacity and the incentives to recruit and develop talent, and ensure everyone in the organization knows they have a role to play in recruiting and training new hires. Building this type of culture did not take place overnight. The team essentially had to go slow to go fast.

Based on our Growth Gauntlet assessment, it was clear their organization was underdeveloped in Elevate Talent relative to other imperatives. They had to build the talent culture, processes, and practices to meet the demands of growth. They had to ensure their sustainability by developing the organizational competency to source, hire, and train talent to meet the demands of business; in short, they built a self-replicating talent machine.

Intentional Onboarding

The first time Meg went to work for a start-up, her onboarding consisted of someone showing her an empty desk and tracking down an IT staffer to give her an email address and a computer. By contrast, when she started a job at an investment bank, she sat through an entire day of very boring paperwork, fingerprinting, and compliance lectures before being shown her desk. And at Google, she flew to the Mountain View campus for an entire week, was made to wear a propeller beanie hat, and was introduced as a "noogler" at the TGIF all-hands meeting. The right formula for onboarding new hires lies somewhere between ignored, bored, and humiliated.

Onboarding is a key opportunity to set new hires up for success. It should be an ongoing process that lasts at least three months and includes three key facets: operational, functional, and cultural.

Operational onboarding refers to the set of tasks or actions that must happen for all new hires to join the company's operations. It includes things like getting an email address, a computer, and a desk, enrolling in payroll and benefits, and completing any other relevant paperwork. These tasks are usually driven by HR, IT, and Security and are completed within the new hire's first few days.

Functional onboarding addresses the learning curve for an employee's specific role or job function. This set of tasks, activities, and trainings differs by employee based on their role. For example, when a new hire starts in sales, they will need to learn the processes, systems, and sales pitches before they can produce. These learning activities are usually managed by the sales leader and take place over several weeks to a few months. Aside from learning how to navigate the organization's processes and systems effectively to get work done, functional onboarding helps new hires establish their internal network. Give new hires a list of key people in other departments they are likely to interact with in the course of their job. Over the next few months, task the new hire with reaching out and scheduling introductory meetings with these key people. This is particularly important for remote employees who may not encounter fellow employees at the watercooler.

Cultural onboarding is an intentional indoctrination into the company's culture and values. It may begin on day one as a formal presentation during the operational onboarding and continue throughout the course of the first few months. It can also happen informally at casual social events, all-hands meetings, or any other time people gather. These interactions allow new hires to witness how people behave with one another, to form relationships, and to learn how work gets done. Without intentional cultural onboarding, new hires may feel like outsiders for longer than necessary and may take longer to get to full productivity. True success comes from knowing more than how to log in to the shared drive; it comes from a sense of belonging and a sense of connectivity to the culture and the people.

HR's Evolving Role in Elevating Talent

If you're going to build a self-replicating talent machine, you are going to need HR. Ever wonder why HR always starts out reporting to the CFO? The role of HR evolves as the company grows and the focus shifts. In the beginning, the basic HR tasks are things like payroll, compensation, benefits, and ensuring the foundational policies are in place to comply with federal and local laws. We call these largely transactional tasks "defense" as they are mostly focused on risk mitigation. These tasks are mission critical, and they are table stakes for a business with employees. In the early days, these tasks may be performed by a bunch of different people across the organization.

As the organization grows beyond 50 employees, employment regulations change, and it's time to hire the first dedicated HR employee. Still largely focused on risk management, the first HR hire most often reports to the leader of the Finance and Accounting function, who oversees payroll, benefits, and so on.

When the company starts growing quickly, a critical shift occurs: Talent becomes a significant part of the business strategy. That's when HR moves out of "defense" and into "offense" with a focus on talent management. It's also when HR moves from being largely *transactional* to *transformational*. At this stage, we start to see HR adding headcount focused on recruiting and performance management, and employee relations and engagement. And perhaps most importantly, HR earns a seat at the leadership table and moves out from under Finance.

A strong HR leader and team are invaluable to a growing organization. HR leaders and their teams are the following:

- Culture ambassadors for the company
- Empathetic problem-solvers who provide a shoulder to cry on when employees deal with personal issues
- Coaches to middle managers on conflict resolution, giving feedback, and so on
- Fingers on the pulse of employee engagement
- Sounding boards for the C-suite tackling complex people issues related to promotions, compensation, legal issues, etc.
- Providers of people-related data
- Conduits to employment attorneys for legal advice
- Purveyors of spirit and morale, hosting fun events to lift spirits and build cohesion
- Strategic partners with a lens on all things people-related
- Talent spotters sourcing, recruiting, training, and promoting talent
- People process builders who know how to involve employees in tasks like interviewing, training, mentoring, and knowledge sharing

And so much more! We have seen companies resist bringing on their first HR hire only to later sheepishly confess that they could not live without them. In our humble opinion, it's never too early to bring in an HR professional. An investment in HR signals to your team that you truly value your people.

Evolution of Human Resources

Emerge	Operationalize	Thrive	Explore & Expand
No dedicated HR employees	First dedicated HR staff hired	HR grows to include strategic talent management focus	A robust HR department exists and plays an important strategic role in talent and risk management
HR tasks are focused on risk management (payroll, benefits, legal)	HR is still mostly related to risk management and is highly transactional	HR team grows to multiple employees, some in risk management, some in talent management	Subspecialties like HRIS, compensation and benefits groups exist
HR tasks are performed by multiple people in the organization	HR reports to Finance/Accounting leader	HR leader may be elevated to leadership team	CHRO is highly strategic and valued
	HR begins to take on talent management tasks		

Elevating Talent across the Four Stages of the Growth Gauntlet

When an organization is in the Emerge stage, talent is convenient. To state it another way, when resources are scarce, you take what you can get. It's not uncommon to see spouses working together: one-half of the partnership is the entrepreneur, and the other invoices the customers. Siblings get roped into the act: one manages product and the other sales. Most of the talent at an early-stage company has one thing in common: a close relationship with the founder. These people play a very important role. They validate the founder's idea and jump on board to help make it happen. These first followers love the idea and the entrepreneur so much they are willing to work for peanuts and the promise of equity that just might be worth something one day.

In the early days, almost everyone in the company is a generalist: someone who has a broad skill set and can manage multiple tasks. Think "chief cook and bottle washer." Everyone has a robust set of responsibilities. Everyone pitches in to get the work done, whatever the work is. (When Meg was head of HR for a start-up, her job included compensation, benefits, recruiting a CEO, and doing the monthly Costco run for snacks.)

As the company evolves into the Operationalize stage and resources are less scarce, more people are added. The early employees shed some of their many hats and start to specialize, presumably in an area where they have developed a skill set or deep institutional knowledge. New hires tend to be more specialized and less convenient. Instead of needing a warm body who will work for peanuts, you may need to do a national search for someone who can recruit and manage a software development team.

The Operationalize stage tends to be an inflection point where many early staffers exit and are replaced by new, more experienced people from outside the organization. At some point, many hit a ceiling in their ability to grow into the specialists the business needs. Growth can feel like musical chairs to those early employees, who are sometimes left without a seat.

One of the biggest challenges for organizations moving from the Emerge to the Operationalize stage is holding poor performers accountable. As roles evolve and shift, some employees may fail to grow or meet the demands of what is necessary for the business. When people fail to level up, it's time to set them free. Layering in performance management processes helps to set clear expectations and ensure people are not surprised when the role diverges from their skills and capabilities. Often performance conversations lead to self-reflection and self-selection out of the role or the organization altogether. It can be incredibly painful to say goodbye to those early folks whose sweat equity built the company.

On the other hand, homegrown talent who can and will scale with the business is priceless. These are the people who carry the company's culture, history, and institutional knowledge. They also tend to have strong relationship capital across the organization and know how to get things done.

Experienced outside hires are also incredibly valuable. Outside hires come into the business with fresh energy, a fresh perspective, and industry best practices that will help the organization grow to the next stage. When a new person starts, they tend to ask questions and politely challenge the status quo, which, when the rest of the team is willing to listen, helps to strengthen the organization.

The Thrive stage is characterized by having the organizational competency (skills, processes, practices, capacity) to bring in talent and get them up to speed quickly to perform their function and add value. Well-worn processes exist to recruit, hire, train, and manage performance. Also, at this stage, a strong middle manager layer is in place to serve as recruiters and trainers of talent, conduits of communication and culture, and continuity for more senior managers. At this stage, the company does not miss a beat when one or even several people exit the team at once. That's what a solid, sustainable, scalable foundation looks like, and it's one that is prepared to grow organically or inorganically.

When the company reaches the Explore and Expand stage, the organization has matured its talent practices and demonstrates the consistent ability to attract and retain talent long term. In this phase, you will see dedicated learning and development teams and programs, succession planning practices, and likely a renewed emphasis on innovation. Many organizations in this stage initiate innovation teams, challenges, and rewards to reinforce the entrepreneurial spirit responsible for the company's original success. Companies that fail to innovate in this stage may begin to decline. Opportunities for growth and innovation are not only important to investors; they also inspire and ultimately retain top talent.

Leveling Up: The Strategic Edge

Critical Questions for the CEO to Ask the Leadership Team

1. Are we devoting enough time on the front end of the hiring process to developing the right role and aligning stakeholders around it?

2. Are we future focused when hiring?

3. Does our onboarding include operational, functional, and cultural training?

4. Is our performance management process driving results or is it a cursory look-back?

5. Are we tolerating poor performers?

6. Do our employees have enough capacity to participate in hiring and training new people?

7. Have we defined what it means to manage (elevate talent) at our company?

Critical Questions for the Board to Ask the CEO

1. Is the organization able to attract and retain top talent? Why or why not?

2. Is developing talent a priority, and are the appropriate resources being allocated to it?

3. Are any poor performers at the leadership level holding the company back?

4. Is talent a multiplier or a limiting factor?

Milestones and Initiatives

- Establish scorecards for each position to be used in hiring and performance management that can be regularly reviewed and updated.

- Develop an onboarding program that includes operational, functional, and cultural training.

- Establish a performance management process that reinforces culture and includes a discussion of performance feedback and forward-looking career goals.

- Define management practices and train all managers on them.

- Build a "self-replicating talent machine."

Elevate Talent Quick Reference

Stages of Growth			
Emerge Informal, Ad Hoc, Undefined, Reactive	**Operationalize** Defined, Data-Informed, Focused, Proactive	**Thrive** Accountable, Data-Driven, Predictable	**Explore & Expand** Strategic, Agile, Innovative, Opportunistic
Talent is convenient, largely hired and managed by founder. Loyalty is valued over accountability. People know who poor performers are, but there is no process or accountability in place to address them.	More experienced and specialized skills are needed. Performance and accountability are increasingly important. Individual contributors are elevated to managers. HR exists and is mostly transactional.	Organization is building core competencies in recruiting, hiring, developing, and liberating talent. Middle managers are consistently trained and accountable for their team's performance. HR adds strategic talent management function.	Strong leadership and talent pipelines exist. Middle managers are key to driving growth, innovation, and engagement. CHRO is elevated to the leadership team.

What is it?

- Hire
- Develop
- Liberate

What's the value?

Talent refers to the people who drive results. Becoming a "self-replicating talent machine" ensures that the business can execute.

CHAPTER 6

Align Structures

"Structure is essential in building anything that thrives."

—Henry Cloud

STRUCTURE FOLLOWS STRATEGY. If you take one thing away from this book, remember that. Harvard Business School professor Alfred DuPont Chandler built an entire management theory around this phrase in 1962, and it's been a guiding mantra in our business.

It was this mantra that led Meg to make what was likely her greatest contribution to her hometown: adding one box to an org chart. While working with a newly elected first-time mayor on his transition, Meg noticed the city's org chart provided for city services like solid waste, public works, libraries, parks, and engineering—all of which reported to a COO. Although mission critical functions of city government, these services had very little to do with the platform the mayor ran on. Who would be tasked with moving his key priorities forward—those things that mattered urgently to voters? Who would make progress on economic development, reducing crime, and providing workforce development opportunities for youth?

The org chart, it seemed to Meg, was structured for "defense" to maintain the city's infrastructure and services. But, it had no "offense." In other words, while someone woke up every day concerned about trash pickup and roadwork, no one woke up thinking about reducing poverty, fighting crime, and attracting businesses to the city. For the mayor to achieve his strategy, he needed someone to run offense. So, they created a chief strategy officer position to oversee the mayor's priorities and ensure these primary objectives had ownership, resources, and stood on more equal footing with the very important city services. This seemingly small change brought the city's structure in line with the mayor's strategy.

When we're called in to help a company scale, one of our primary concerns is whether the structure is aligned with and supports the strategy. When we think about structure, we think not only about the org chart, but also the systems and processes that support the strategy. Structures aid in achieving goals because they clarify roles, create accountability, and provide boundaries between functions, all of which build trust. Processes are designed to advance work through the organization and push it out to clients/customers. Systems help to track and measure progress to optimize performance.

The question you have to answer is, what kind of structure will help you achieve your strategy? For example, if the strategy is to grow revenue by 50 percent in 12 months, the structure to support the strategy might include the following:

- Building out sales and customer success teams

- Shoring up operational processes to handle a larger volume of customers

- Building out talent recruitment systems to bring in new salespeople quickly

- Reducing redundancies to mitigate risk at single points of failure
- Upgrading technology systems
- Reworking sales compensation to incentivize revenue growth more heavily
- Investing in marketing

Each function has a role to play in achieving the strategy. Once you've identified those goals, look at the team. Does the team have the skills, knowledge, and experience to do what it takes to achieve the goals? If not, what skills, knowledge, or expertise do you need to hire?

The Strategic Table

We call the Executive Leadership Team in a high-growth company the Strategic Table. The Strategic Table is the group that has the collective ownership of the company's strategy. They possess the expertise and perspective to guide the business, and they have the authority and purview over the resources, financial and people, to execute.

Over time, the leaders at the Strategic Table may change as the organization grows and its strategy changes. For example, a retail chain's survival was dependent on making the shift to an omnichannel model. They realized that this transformational strategic shift required looking outside to hire an executive with proven experience in e-commerce and digital marketing. The new executive owned that piece of the business strategy and built an e-commerce team to support omnichannel and lead the transformation. He was an essential addition to the executive team.

Many executive teams suffer from bloat as the company grows.

CEOs, especially founders, tend to only add positions to the team as they are reluctant to demote those early employees. Eventually, the leadership team grows too big and unwieldy and you'll need to right-size. When you do, here are some design principles for the Strategic Table to guide you:

- Size matters. Keep the team to nine people or fewer permanent members. Any more than that makes it difficult to build trust and engage in robust discussion.

- Overweight the team with a slightly greater number of experts in the company's products, services, and revenue than leaders in operations and support. This tip from Google's Eric Schmidt ensures that the risk managers don't completely stifle the growth plans of the risk-takers.

- Ensure that collectively the team has responsibility for the entirety of the organization. As you make resource decisions, you want to have everyone you need at the table to both inform and execute on those decisions.

- Establish ownership. Be sure that everyone at the table knows exactly which part of the strategy they are responsible for, and, further, be sure that all key strategic initiatives have an owner at the table. For example, if your strategy calls for doubling the number of employees you have in a year, you need HR at the table.

- Strategic, forward-focused, mission-aligned leaders only. Those on the leadership team must come with an enterprise-wide perspective. Leaders representing their individual functions and agendas stand in the way of progress.

A tech-enabled healthcare company had an ambitious strategy that called for significant software development. As we reviewed their Strategic Table, we were perplexed by the fact that the CTO was not on the Executive Leadership Team (ELT). When we raised this issue with the CEO, we learned that the ELT did not believe the CTO was executive level (i.e., he was not strategic enough to be included in senior leadership). As a result, this mission critical piece of their strategy was not represented at the table. Ultimately, what became clear was that they needed to level up by hiring a new CTO who could own the strategy and bring an enterprise-wide technology perspective to the Strategic Table.

Boundaries = Trust

Years ago, the now-famous "Playground Study" was conducted by a team of landscape architects on preschool-age children.[16] The study observed the children playing first on a playground without a fence and later playing on a similar playground with a perimeter fence serving as a boundary. In the first scenario, the children stayed close to the teacher for the duration of play. In the second, the children spread out to the edges of the fenced boundary. The conclusion was boundaries make us feel safe and expand our comfort zone. The children experienced greater freedom and range of movement when a boundary existed. The same is true of organizational structures and processes: Boundaries allow for increased feelings of trust and safety, which promotes exploration and expansion.

For you serial entrepreneurs who read that last sentence and thought, "Boundaries stifle creativity! Who needs boundaries?" let us continue. The second most important thing to remember about structures is they are dynamic and ever-changing. As a company grows and the strategy evolves, so must the structures. Unlike a playground fence, leaders have the ability to shift boundaries and structures to meet the demands of their specific situation.

For highly entrepreneurial organizations in the Emerge stage, the "area of play" might be quite large with lots of room to roam and explore. In later stages, when the focus shifts to operationalizing products and services, the parameters will likely become tighter and more defined to promote consistency and quality. The key is to know what your strategy is and what stage of the Growth Gauntlet you're in to determine what kinds of structures are right for your organization.

Another way to think about structure is as a means to manifest trust in an organization. During the Emerge stage, when there is very little structure, trust is cultivated among team members who form close working relationships. As the organization grows and adds more people, it becomes impossible to have the same level of trust or the same number of close relationships with everyone you need to rely on. Systems and processes serve as a proxy for trust in that we learn to trust these structures, even when we don't necessarily know the person completing each of the steps along the way.

For example, one such process is the checks and balances set up to ensure proper financial controls. Steps in the process, such as requiring dual signatures on checks and imposing spending limits and prior approvals for big expenditures, ensure that no one person has too much authority. Employees know where the fence line is and what the rules are. The value of building these repeatable processes aligned with your strategy is in knowing and trusting the work will be accomplished within the established time and resource parameters.

During our yearlong engagement with a client, we noticed a phenomenon around meetings. We would schedule a meeting with the key decision-makers on a topic, and those decision-makers would invite others on their teams to join. Often, we showed up to lead a discussion with what we thought would be five people, only to find fifteen at the table! This happened so often that we had to explicitly ask the key decision-makers *not* to invite anyone else.

We determined there was a lack of trust in the organization, both in the culture and the organizational structure. The solution was not more people at every meeting—a frustrating and work-stifling experience—but defining roles, boundaries, and decision-making authority. When the team members collaboratively set the boundaries and were empowered to enforce those boundaries, they were able to trust they could live with decisions made in meetings they did not attend.

When you begin to experience departmental silos, communication challenges, and accountability issues, chances are you've got an organizational design issue. To be effective, an organizational structure must align with the company's business goals and shift when those goals change. The goal of organizational design is to identify the optimal structure for an organization to operate efficiently and effectively to meet its goals.

According to the authors of *Organizational Design: A Step-by-Step Approach*, the fundamentals to consider are as follows:[17]

1. Goals

2. Tasks

3. Decision-making authority

4. Communication

5. Incentives

We take this model one step further and add *culture* to the fundamentals of organizational design. You have to consider the culture when designing your structure.

Silicon Valley tech companies are notoriously flat, with very few layers of management between the engineers and the executives. The purpose of this flat organizational structure is to encourage free information flow as a means to unleash innovation: a competitive business strategy and a cultural attribute of the company.

In contrast, the US armed services is organized by a command-and-control structure with well-defined and enforced hierarchy, as we touched upon in Chapter 3. The military prioritizes decision-making authority over the free flow of information. Both tech companies and the armed forces are organized to reach their specific goals efficiently and effectively, but their structures are extremely different. The organizational structure of each operation supports their overall strategies and aligns with their culture.

Structuring for Innovation

As we mentioned in Chapter 1, there are two types of innovation: Innovation with a capital "I" and innovation with a lowercase "i." Capital I Innovation refers to transformative inventions or strategic redirection. They are the investments a company makes in the long-term future of the business and the external forces that may impact it. These formal, leadership-driven Innovation efforts include activities like holding off-sites to engage in strategic "blue ocean" thinking: establishing formal teams to study and pursue new product lines, markets, and technologies; and/or hiring new executives, such as a chief innovation officer, to lead the way. Companies may create internal accelerators or incubators to encourage creative teams to experiment with ideas and prove out concepts, or they may acquire a start-up or small company that is already pursuing a great idea. And sometimes, investing in Innovation requires resourcing and restructuring the team to reflect its business stage as it transitions from Operationalize to Growth or Explore and Expand.

CASE IN POINT: ADAPTING STRUCTURE TO GROWTH NEEDS

In an effort to accelerate their autonomous vehicles efforts and compete with other major automakers, General Motors (GM) acquired Cruise, a Silicon Valley start-up, in 2016. Cruise's culture and methods were antithetical to the large, mature, and bureaucratic behemoth GM had become. Leadership rightly understood the nimble start-up would be crushed under the full weight of GM's complex structure and multiple layers of leadership, processes, and systems. They decided to leave the Cruise team as a stand-alone entity in Silicon Valley but empowered them to access any resources necessary from the parent company. The decision regarding the structure protected the autonomy and flexibility of Cruise's Innovative arm, allowing them to move faster and experiment.

GM CEO Mary Barra had the foresight to recognize the positive influence Cruise's entrepreneurial team might have on the staid culture at GM. She was quoted in *Fast Company* instructing the Cruise team, "If somebody [at GM] says you can't have something, or you can't do something, or it's going to take this much time, and it doesn't make sense to you, challenge them. I want to take the energy and speed of how you look at doing things and drive it into the core of GM."[18]

Resourcing Innovation can be tricky. Former Google CEO Eric Schmidt and former VP of products Jonathan Rosenberg refer to the 70/20/10 rule in their 2014 book, *How Google Works*. They say

70 percent of a company's capacity should be dedicated to the core activities that sustain the business, and the remaining 30 percent of capacity and resources should be put toward Innovation efforts. Of that 30 percent, 20 percent of those emerging initiatives will achieve some level of early success and have real potential, while 10 percent will fall into the category of the higher risk, brand-new ventures. "While the 70/20/10 rule ensured that our core business would always get the bulk of the resources, the promising, up-and-coming areas would also get investment. The crazy ideas got some support too, and were protected from the inevitable budget cuts," they said.

On the flip side, lowercase "i" innovation refers to incremental changes that increase efficiency and effectiveness. This type of innovation is generally grassroots-led and flows from the bottom up. Ideas bubble from the front line, where people experience bottlenecks, waste, and customer dissatisfaction firsthand. From this vantage point, they are able to identify opportunities for improvement.

Lowercase innovation may have less wow factor than its counterpart, but it tends to be immediately impactful. Critically, it requires the structure, culture, and communication channels that allow for ideas to surface from deep within the organization and make their way up the chain to leadership for formal adoption and recognition.

Everyone in an organization has the potential to innovate from where they sit and should be readily encouraged to do so. You can foster this type of innovation by emphasizing a culture of continuous improvement and rewarding those whose efforts make a significant contribution to the bottom line. Rewarding incremental innovations, as well as big leaps, keeps all facets of the business healthy and relevant. The long-term success of a mature business depends on balancing both types of innovation.

Structuring for Accountability

We recently met with a board member and investor in an emerging company about some headwinds the company was facing. As we talked, we realized the company had fallen out of the regular discipline of quarterly board meetings, and the board's visibility into the operations had become stale. There was a growing concern about underperformance in sales. We thought the first step was to get the company back on track with regular meetings and perhaps add a mid-quarter update call to our routine.

Everyone in an organization has the potential to innovate from where they sit.

The power of a board meeting is not necessarily about what is accomplished in the meeting; the real power lies in what is accomplished in preparation for the meeting. We've all been there. Everyone wants to report good progress to the board. As the board meeting date approaches, the whole team shifts into overdrive to demonstrate strong results. When meetings fall off the schedule, so does accountability.

Meg tries to throw a dinner party every six months, at least, so she'll clean the house. It's amazing what the threat of someone coming to dinner will motivate you to do: removing clutter that you've overlooked for months. Think of board meetings as a dinner party with your toughest critics who will give your organization the white glove test. Regular board meetings, or any meeting for that matter, provide a structure that creates forward momentum.

Pat Lencioni, famous for his leadership fables, wrote about how companies can improve the efficacy of their internal meetings to create better accountability in *Death by Meeting*. In his 2004 book, he outlines four different types of meetings: daily check-ins, tactical staff meetings, ad hoc topical meetings, and quarterly strategy reviews.

Daily check-ins are short, informal, and administrative. Tactical staff meetings last longer, perhaps an hour, and allow for discussion of issues and obstacles. Park any strategic topics that surface and require more discussion for an ad hoc topical meeting where the team can bring their creative minds to discuss, analyze, and brainstorm. And finally, quarterly strategic reviews offer an opportunity to get out of the weeds of the day-to-day operations and focus on the overall business strategy. These quarterly off-sites may take one to two days.

It's important to note that each of these meetings has a distinct purpose. We've all been in endless staff meetings when someone derails the agenda with an ad hoc topic, or a strategic off-site that wanders into a tactical discussion. Hold the line on the purpose of the meeting and park those discussions for their appropriate forum. Keep meetings on time. Provide agendas ahead of the meeting and meeting notes afterward. When you are in the habit of practicing these aspects of meeting hygiene, you will see your team's accountability improve.

Without structured systems for accountability, the danger of failing to meet key milestones and initiatives becomes greater, reminiscent of the following old anecdote:

There was an important job to be done, and Everybody was sure that Somebody would do it. Anybody could have done it, but Nobody did it. Somebody got angry because it was Everybody's job. Everybody thought that Anybody could do it, but Nobody realized that Everybody wouldn't do it. It ended up that Everybody blamed Somebody when Nobody did what Anybody could have done.[19]

Avoid the common trap of falling into a maddening riddle and ensure your structures promote clarity, accountability, transparency, and ownership.

SINGLE POINTS OF FAILURE

Many structural systems, processes, and protocols are the result of solving pain points. Meg's attorney husband always says, "Every rule has someone's name on it." Think about the TSA security checkpoint. All of the prohibited or screened items can be traced back to someone who tried to use that item to cause harm, including shoes. The same tends to be true—though with less dangerous consequences—with how and why we structure our organizations. Although our core tenet is "people drive results," people can also put an organization at risk.

When we're evaluating a company's structures, one key risk factor we look for is whether there are any single points of failure, where one employee owns a critical function, and there is no one else with the same level of skill or knowledge who can stand in for them if necessary.

Real-world examples of such a risk include the following:

- A highly skilled engineer who built a proprietary software system and is the only person who can troubleshoot when it goes down
- The finance person who is the sole signatory on key accounts
- The account manager who has a high concentration of key account relationships and owns a disproportionate percentage of revenue

In rare cases, one person might be a dual point of failure—take the church organist who was also the IT guy. Talk about a unicorn!

When we identify these mission critical people, our goal is to mitigate the risk should they exit unexpectedly. Solutions don't always necessitate adding another person to the team, though if the budget permits, it's not a bad idea. There are several action steps to create redundancy and reduce harm, and they can be as varied as people's responsibilities. In the case of the engineer with the proprietary system, thorough documentation helps ensure someone else can learn the system. Financial controls should always be established with a checks-and-balances approach, dual signatories, and oversight. For the account manager holding the keys to the majority of key relationships, a revamped team approach ensures client relationships extend beyond one person to others in the company. Also, be sure to have key people share client information and that important account information is kept up to date in a centralized system.

Does your business have any immediately recognizable single points of failure? They tend to be more predominant in Emerge or Operationalize stage companies, where a single individual knows "everything about X," and the business will come to a standstill if Johnny in payroll gets sick or Lucy in product development is unable to complete a proprietary deliverable she alone designed. Who has ownership over your key business functions, and who else knows how to operate them in their absence?

Structuring Compensation

"Structure follows strategy" is also an important mantra when it comes to structuring compensation. To design an effective compensation program, you need to first understand the business strategy. Compensation, after all, is meant to incentivize and reward the behaviors that lead to the company's success. Therefore, we need to understand what kinds of behavior drive the desired results and thus what we want to incentivize and reward. Should we put a higher percentage of our sales team's compensation at risk to spur business development? Should we inspire people to collaborate with one another or reward individual performance? How might we motivate those who are excellent at customer service? These are the types of questions that contribute to building an effective compensation structure.

Structure follows strategy.

Meg stepped into the role of Compensation Committee Chair for an emerging company in the midst of some conflict. Investors had a practice of paying bonuses to the management team based on the company's performance. The challenge was that the payouts were largely discretionary, determined at the end of the year after a board discussion and some reflection on the year. It was a no-win situation. No expectations had been set, so none were met. It seemed like everyone was unhappy at year-end.

When Meg stepped into the role, the first order of business was to establish a structure and methodology for paying bonuses. The goal was for both the management team and the investors to have clarity at the beginning of the year on the company's goals and what the payout would be for outsized performance. It took some haggling to get everyone to agree to a satisfactory plan.

Ultimately, everyone agreed on two components:

1. Employees should be rewarded for their individual performance.

2. Everyone should participate in the upside if the company had a great year.

With that, they designed a two-tier bonus structure in which 50 percent of an employee's bonus was tied to their individual performance measured by achieving their unique goals, and 50 percent of their bonus was directly tied to the company hitting its annual revenue target. The structure incentivized employees to perform individually and collectively as a team to contribute to the company's growth. It also put a fine point on the revenue goals as the most important priority.

This structure made the year-end comp committee a lot easier. With expectations set and a formula in place, they just had to plug in the numbers to calculate bonuses. The board did reserve some discretion, but by and large, they stuck with the agreed-upon structure. The second year the plan was in place, the strategy changed. Investors believed the company needed to focus on a specific subset of revenue—selling the inventory they already had versus buying new inventory. So, they modified the bonus structure to prioritize sales of the existing inventory over the new product. Again, though, they set the formula and the goals at the beginning of the year to incentivize the work. The company blew the target out of the water. And, that year, everyone was happy.

If you have a bonus and incentive comp plan, you can avoid misunderstandings and unmet expectations and, most importantly, motivate strong performance by adopting a structure that sets clear expectations and aligns with company goals.

Aligning Structure across the Four Stages of the Growth Gauntlet

Strategy, number of people, and complexity are the biggest drivers of change in organizational structure. In the Emerge stage, the focus is on proving the concept: Can we do this?

In the Operationalize stage, the focus shifts to, can we do this every time? Developing the organizational competency to execute on the product or service reliably and predictably requires more structure and process.

At the Operationalize stage, the organization expands, and departments emerge to specialize in functions such as product development, sales, customer support, finance, HR, and so on. Each function has a specific role in sustaining and growing the business. Basically, you are building the foundational structure that moves the product or service through the system. There's a strong internal focus at this point in the company's life as leaders work to build the infrastructure needed to grow.

The Thrive stage begins when you turn on the water to see if the pipes work. With the infrastructure in place, the question becomes, can we do this at scale? How much water can we move through the plumbing without bursting the pipes? Most companies build out their product or service implementation at the same time they build out a sales force. Don't let Sales turn on the spigot until the operations are ready to handle the influx. The market momentum generated by sales has to be matched by sturdy operations that can meet the demand. Many companies have drowned after failing to adequately prepare for growth.

At the Explore and Expand stage, conventional wisdom suggests mature businesses must innovate or die. The accelerated pace of technological disruption puts companies under increasing pressure to innovate; both capital "I" and lowercase "i" innovation are necessary for survival.

Leveling Up: The Strategic Edge

Critical Questions for the CEO to Ask the Leadership Team

1. Do we have any single points of failure?

2. Does our leadership team meet the design principles for the Strategic Table?

3. Does our structure promote innovation/Innovation?

4. Is our compensation structured to incentivize our strategy?

Critical Questions for the Board to Ask the CEO

1. Does the company have any single points of failure, and if so, how will we address those?

2. Does the leadership team meet the design principles for the Strategic Table?

3. Does the team need to add critical skills and experience to execute on their strategy?

4. Where does innovation live?

Milestones and Initiatives

- Identify single points of failure and mitigate risks.
- Assess your leadership team based on the design principles for the Strategic Table.
- Test compensation structures for alignment with strategy.
- Establish structures to promote innovation.

Align Structures Quick Reference

Stages of Growth			
Emerge Informal, Ad Hoc, Undefined, Reactive	**Operationalize** Defined, Data-Informed, Focused, Proactive	**Thrive** Accountable, Data-Driven, Predictable	**Explore & Expand** Strategic, Agile, Innovative, Opportunistic
Organization is structured as one undefined team largely all reporting to the founder. Manual processes emerge.	Functional structure is defined. Departments emerge. Processes are being formalized, defined, documented.	Structure is aligned with strategy. Repeatable processes are in place driven by systems, tools, and automation.	Structure is agile and evolves with strategy. Processes are mined for efficiencies, continuous improvement.

What is it?

- Org Chart
- Processes
- Systems
- Policies

What's the value?

When aligned with the strategy, structures provide the scaffolding to support growth and scale.

CHAPTER 7

Amplify Communication

"Communication is the lifeblood of any organization,
and without it, the organization will wither and die."

—Peter F. Drucker

COMMUNICATION POWERS A CEO'S journey through the Growth Gauntlet. It electrifies the grid. It's the energy that organizations run on. Communication brings the other five Imperatives to life, so, its importance cannot be overstated. Effective communication drives higher employee morale, engagement, and retention. The global advisory firm Towers Watson found companies with highly effective communication practices had 47 percent higher shareholder returns compared to those with poor communication practices.[20] Good communication practices foster clarity, alignment, and trust—essential elements for every organization.

Jason was the CEO of a company that owned numerous apartment complexes. Upon interviewing leaders from the properties, we discovered simmering frustration with him for his lack of capital investment in the properties. Worse, employees felt he had promised to make improvements but had not followed through. When we relayed this feedback to Jason, he became visibly upset and stormed out of the room. A few moments later, he returned with his laptop. He spun it around to show us a spreadsheet totaling nearly $20 million he had systematically invested in the properties. He was both disappointed and angry about the employees' comments, and his first reaction was to draft a company-wide email to quash the rumors.

As we talked further with him and dug into why there existed such a disconnect, he began to realize he had not made a habit of communicating about the improvements to the whole company. Only the properties that were actively being improved had any knowledge of the work he was doing. And further, he had future improvements planned that had not yet been communicated. Jason came to understand he was missing a huge opportunity by not communicating to his team. Not only was Jason not getting the credit for investing; his team was disappointed in him as well. They had a negative opinion of him because they lacked information. The good news was this circuit could be easily connected and shine a bright light on the positive work he was doing. As George Bernard Shaw is believed to have said, "The single biggest problem in communication is the illusion that it has taken place."

The Purpose of Communication

A big part of any successful CEO's role is communication, and as your organization progresses through the Four Stages of the Growth Gauntlet, communication requires a greater percentage of a CEO's time and energy. Leaders must develop the skills to communicate effectively in all directions, from the top down and the bottom up, to the leadership team, to the middle managers, and to the entire organization. They must be effective in delivering tough messages in person to employees in a one-on-one meeting and onstage to large groups of employees, shareholders, and likely the press.

As a leader, what you say and how you say it matters. Communication is not a one-size-fits-all discipline. In the same way we use electricity for various purposes in our homes, successful leaders wield communication for many different reasons: to inform, educate, inspire, engage, and connect.

INFORM

Information comes in many shapes and sizes: data, announcements, news, research, emails, and so on. Employees across the company make small decisions every day that impact the business strategy. The better equipped they are with the information they need to do their jobs, the more effective they can be. Communication of information must be frequent and timely. As with electricity, it's important to have the right amount of information. Too little, and the circuit won't connect, leaving people in the dark and unable to perform to their potential. Too much, and the circuit will overload, leading to the same result—the inability to perform.

One of our favorite descriptions of a particular leader by a board member was, "When you ask him what time it is, he'll build you a watch." Make no mistake he is a brilliant and talented guy, but his communication style overwhelms and bores his peers, and, worse, his board. He once delivered a presentation to his board, and at the end of the two hours, the board chair said, "All of that went completely over my head. All we need to know is what the plan is." And the rest of the room agreed. He was not asked back to present again.

Providing too much detail can be as counterproductive as not providing enough.

Living in the information age has its drawbacks. We have so much information at our fingertips that it's hard to cut through the noise and focus on what we really need. Curating that information and providing clarity to employees is an important organizational competency to develop.

EDUCATE

Communicating to educate is about knowledge transfer. It's deeper and more complex than simply sharing information. It might include a repository of institutional knowledge, training sessions, and/or onboarding—basically, wherever and however learning takes place. We tend to think of information as a resource that is consumed in smaller bits and knowledge as something more complex to be learned. Employees must be constantly educated on everything from best practices for doing their jobs to industry and market trends that impact their work.

Educational communication takes many forms: brown bag lunches, training sessions, mentoring, outside speakers, access to experts, and so on. Google used to post short, educational material in the bathroom stalls! Successful leaders are constantly asking, "What does our organization need to get smart on?" or "How do we level up our knowledge to stay relevant?" And, as we discussed in Chapter 5, "How do we transfer knowledge to new hires to quickly get them to up productivity?"

INSPIRE

Inspirational communication is vital for cultural connection and alignment. It is critical to win the hearts and minds of employees so they are excited about working for the organization. Leaders are responsible for inspiring their teams, for motivating them to action to meet a challenge, for celebrating collective wins, and for recognizing individual accomplishments. Inspirational communication connects the employees to the culture of the organization and aims to make them feel both valued and a part of something bigger than themselves.

Many years ago, when Meg was at Google, the then-CEO Eric Schmidt visited the office in Santa Monica to connect with the team and inform them of new initiatives. Before he went out to address the employees, he asked her for an update on the office. She told him that a beloved young systems administrator, JJ Feick, had passed away suddenly, and the team was grieving over this terrible loss. Eric sat down and asked several questions about JJ. A few minutes later, when he took the stage to address the 100-person team, he delivered heartfelt words about JJ. Though Eric was something of a celebrity CEO, his inspirational talk and genuine empathy for the team over their loss of a cherished colleague humanized him, and, as a result, the group felt a unique connection to him. Perhaps most importantly, they felt valued, and they felt JJ's contributions and impact were valued as well. His ability to quickly pivot and prioritize empathy, respect, and warmth for JJ and the team over the informational communication he had come to deliver was awe inspiring. It was a master class in the power of inspirational communication.

ENGAGE

Utilizing communication for its power to engage is frequently overlooked or undervalued. Given the amount of effort devoted to communicating to inform, educate, and inspire, leaders tend to focus on what they communicate out to employees. Communicating for engagement, on the other hand, is all about listening and taking in information. Getting feedback from employees spurs insights on everything from morale to innovation and efficiency. Frontline employees are the experts on what they do each day. Leaders who want to have their finger on the pulse of the organization will find multiple ways to engage with their employees, listen to their perspectives, and absorb their unique insights.

One of the most effective methods is "Management by Walking Around," which just means taking the time to walk the floor and ask people a few good questions. Don't ask questions that can be answered with "fine." Ask open-ended questions people need to provide a thoughtful response to, such as, "What's something you think I should know, but probably don't, about your work?" or, "If you were in charge, what changes would you make?" or, "If there's one thing that would help you to do your job better, what would it be?" And don't take "I don't know" for an answer. The goal, of course, is to engage employees in a conversation.

One CEO we know used to carry a $100 bill in his pocket. When he traveled to different worksites across the country, he would ask employees at random to recite the core values of the company for him. If they could do it, he gave them $100 on the spot. This form of engagement helped reinforce the company's values and culture. When word got out about this practice, people became more serious about memorizing and living out the values.

Other ways to engage your employees are through formal regular engagement surveys that ask a multitude of questions or through a Net Promoter Score survey, which asks a single question. Both are a good barometer for how people are feeling at the moment. The point is to create space and mechanisms to actively inquire and listen to the organization. What you learn will be invaluable. Critically, once you ask for feedback from your employees, you must take it to heart and circle back to them to say, "This is what I heard, and this is what

I intend to do about it." Certainly, you can't address every small complaint, but you must select a few things from the feedback to take on. Closing the loop in this way lets employees know their feedback is valued. Without this step, they are less likely to provide feedback the next time around or to trust that management will do anything with it.

CONNECT

Just like the electrical grid, the organization is a network. It's made up of people who must connect to get work done, and it requires you to plug in and connect with them.

Once upon a time, in the 1990s, Meg worked for an investment bank. This was back before PowerPoint and Google Slides, when only a select few had access to graphic design programs and could produce the slick presentations that bankers put in front of clients. The select few were in a group called Presentation Technologies, or PresTech, and they stood between you and your deadline. Having someone in PresTech you could call on for help at the last minute was critical. People who failed to build relationships with this team did not fare well.

In addition to fostering the relationships that are critical to success, it's also incredibly important to find a sense of community in the workplace. Gallup engagement surveys consistently find that employees who report having at least one friend at work are happier and more productive than those who do not.[21] Building relationships at work is part of building trust, and trust is necessary for both candor and accountability.

As discussed in Chapter 5, a good onboarding process offers introductions to employees across the company to help new hires build the network they need to do their jobs well. This is particularly important for remote workers who might not have the benefit of meeting people around the office. Mentors and assigned work buddies can also help with introductions and internal networking. The faster a new hire can access the network, the faster they will get to productivity.

ACME COMMUNICATIONS MAP

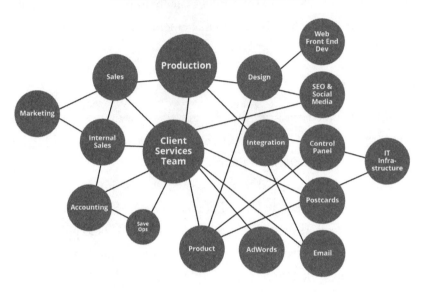

The Multiple Communication Channels and Styles

Back in the dark ages of the '90s, before email and cell phones, communication was slower. The investment firm Meg worked for had a mailroom and a cadre of mailroom employees. They walked the floors of the high-rise each day, pushing a metal cart and distributing mail along with fliers to communicate announcements. The fliers were color coded. A blue sheet of paper was a memo from HR, green was from Finance and Accounting, and if something really *big* was happening, everyone received a goldenrod. Goldenrod is a particular shade of yellow paper stock, and it was reserved for big announcements from the C-suite, like executive promotions or the announcement of a merger. It's funny now to imagine a flier, hot off the presses, and hand delivered to 3,000 people as the fastest mode of communication, but it was an effective method to amplify communication at the time.

Communication methods have evolved significantly over the last two decades, and executives can now rely on multiple channels to amplify their communication and keep their organizations humming. Technology plays a huge role in our current communications landscape, with companies using everything from Slack to CRMs and ERMs to AI chatbots. Organizations that communicate effectively are adept at multidirectional communication, using various channels and technologies, and reinforcing culture through their messaging. Successful leaders will plan their communications by thinking through the purpose, style, and channel that will be most effective at reaching the intended audience. As we think about the Six Imperatives, we can broadly chart the different styles and channels of communication a leader might use for each.

Communication Styles and Channels

		Styles of Communication	Communication Channels
The Six Imperatives	**Sharpen Focus**	Inspire, inform, educate	Meetings, surveys, offsite, broadcasts, strategic plan
	Calibrate Culture	Inspire, connect, engage	Onboarding, town hall, networking, training
	Strengthen Leadership	Connect, engage	Networking, offsite
	Elevate Talent	Connect, educate, engage	Training, onboarding, surveys, job description, performance scorecard
	Align Structures	Inform, connect	Onboarding, org chart
	Amplify Communication	All	All

As you look at the chart, you may be surprised to see "job description" or "strategic plan" listed as communications channels. But, in fact, as we have touched on in previous chapters, these documents (and many others) are important opportunities to share information, reinforce culture, and provide clarity for your team. Our message to CEOs is not to waste a single touch point with employees but to think of each as an opportunity to amplify communication and calibrate culture.

We can think about communication channels in three directional categories: top down, bottom up, and multidirectional. According to the Growth Gauntlet, organizations with the most mature communications functions have robust channels that serve all three.

TOP-DOWN COMMUNICATION

Communication from leadership to the rest of the organization is perhaps the easiest form of communication because it's the one leaders can actually control. As such, it makes sense for leaders to be thoughtful about the content, style, and channels they use.

There's no such thing as overcommunicating. In fact, most people must hear a message seven to eleven times before they internalize it. If you have teenagers, you know what we're talking about! Also, it's important to understand your workforce is made up of people who process information differently. You likely have both visual and auditory processors, which means you'll need to deliver messages in multiple formats: verbal, written, graphically, and so on.

Our chart speaks to the style of communication leaders might use depending on their purpose and which channels might be most effective. For example, if you are sharpening focus by energizing and engaging your team around a strategic plan, you'll want to do so in a high-energy town hall meeting and follow up with a written email broadcast that includes a copy of the strategic plan. Or, if you're elevating talent by providing performance feedback to an employee, you'll want to have a one-on-one meeting and come well prepared with written material to support your message, like a performance feedback summary.

BOTTOM-UP COMMUNICATION

To make the best decisions, spot issues and opportunities, and cultivate ideas, leaders must hear from employees at all levels of the organization. As companies grow, create opportunities for employees to provide feedback and share thoughts and ideas. This might include regular employee surveys, office hours for managers, or regular town hall meetings where employees can ask questions and share feedback.

Hearing employee feedback goes a long way toward making people feel valued. When employees feel heard, they are much more likely to be engaged and have higher morale.

To that end, it is important to create a culture that inspires employees to communicate the information you need to make the best decisions. That means being open to hearing the feedback and acting on it. If employees provide feedback and they perceive no one is doing anything with it, they will stop providing it. And that's game over.

When people give feedback, make suggestions, or offer ideas, actively listen to them. Active listening is listening to understand without responding. Give them your undivided attention and try to learn as much as you can. Be curious. Ask clarifying questions. Doing so will be informative for you and show others you value their input. NFL head coach Brian Daboll describes it this way:

"When you are at this level and people walk through your door to talk to you about something, it is the most important thing on their mind, and it has been bothering them for weeks and they've wanted to talk to you about it, and they finally have the [nerve] to walk in and talk to you."[22]

When people give you feedback, don't get defensive, even (and especially) if it's unsolicited. You may ask clarifying questions to make sure you understand or to get more information, but don't be dismissive, defensive, or demeaning. Reflect on what you've heard, and try to see the situation from their point of view. Often, people's perceptions won't be factually correct because they don't have the whole picture, but that doesn't make them any less real. Their perception is the way they are currently experiencing the company. If knowing the facts would change their perception, you have a great opportunity to share what you know, what you're planning, or your thought process behind a decision.

MULTIDIRECTIONAL COMMUNICATION

In business, people tend to be organized around similar functions and work cooperatively to advance the business strategy: Sales, Marketing, IT, HR, Finance, and so on. The work of any organization requires these functions to communicate with one another. In the field of organizational health, a common theme frequently arises and is described in one word: silos. Silos occur when one or more of the different functions make decisions in an echo chamber without sufficiently coordinating with the other groups. Most often, we find this happens when there is a command-and-control-style leader, or the culture prohibits multidirectional information flow. For example, a culture is focused on individual achievement, and recognition may inadvertently encourage employees to withhold information from others to ensure they get "credit."

A middle manager was in charge of a large and important initiative. The company he worked for had a strong command-and-control culture, and he was restricted from communicating directly with all the people required to advance the initiative. Everything had to go through his superior. When asked by someone in another department to set up a meeting to discuss the initiative, he had to ask for permission from his boss, which added a layer of time delay. This scenario is the very definition of office politics, where people don't have the ability to freely collaborate with others outside of their department. Silos and politics create bottlenecks; they slow, stall, or block advancement. Multidirectional, free communication flow across the organization solves that.

Some leaders might bristle at the thought of free communication flow. And yes, it's true; communication does require some governors, but leaders can establish protocols ahead of time to govern communication flow. Setting up a RACI matrix, for example, helps provide clarity around communication, which empowers employees and allays fears of managers. RACI stands for "Responsible," "Accountable," "Consult," and "Inform." A RACI matrix outlines how communication should flow on a project or initiative, and it specifies who needs to know what and when. At the outset of a project, a team can agree on the role each person will play. The "Responsible" role is likely the person driving the project. The "Accountable" party might be the head of the department who will own the outcome and results. Other stakeholders might be required to "Consult" on the project by providing certain expertise or work product. And still others who are less involved may just want to be "Informed" as the project progresses or hits certain milestones. The RACI matrix helps establish clear expectations and set boundaries on the front end for the multidirectional information flow.

RACI Matrix

Project Plan/ Action Steps	People/Departments				
	Project Manager	Department Head	Employee 1	Employee 2	Employee 3
Project: Onboard employees	R	A	C	C	I
Create agenda	R	I	C	C	I
Reserve conference room	R	I	I	I	I
Communicate with new hires	R	I	I	I	I
Prepare materials	A	I	R	I	I
Present benefits information	A	I	R	I	I
Present IT orientation	A	I	I	R	I
Present company culture and history	A	R	I	I	I

R = Responsible
Performs task in support of effort; responsible for doing the work

A = Accountable
Accountable to be sure the task is carried out and achieves the intended results; initiates, follows through, manages task

C = Consulted
Needs to provide input review, advice, go-no-go, or technical support

I = Informed
Needs to be kept current, but does not have decision input

Communicating through Change

More change and volatility exist in the workplace today than ever before. As uncertainty increases and the dizzying pace of change becomes the norm, the expectations and demands on leaders grow more complex. In high-growth companies, the frequency of change is even greater, and leaders must be able to lead through ambiguity and inspire team buy-in for each new change. This is no small task. Gallup estimates that 70 percent of all change efforts fail to reach their full potential.[23]

Approach change communication from a place of curiosity, empathy, and patience because how you communicate with your team and the entire organization through change is critical. There are numerous tactical change-management processes and templates for structuring and delivering change communications. The most important starting place, however, is your own mindset. Having a growth versus fixed mindset applies here, just as it does in relation to providing feedback (Chapter 4). Leaders tend to assume there will be resistance from employees, so they view comments and reactions through the filter of employees refusing to change. When leaders are in this mindset, they may talk down to their teams or be heavy-handed in their expectations. It's important to recognize initial reactions from employees such as surprise, resistance, or failure to immediately adapt are natural reactions. They do not represent a refusal to accept and adopt the changes, and these reactions are not a personal affront.

Employee reactions to change are similar to an iceberg. There are things you can see on the surface—complaints, grumblings, comments—but the root causes and drivers of these outward reactions are below the surface, and they are often unspoken. Most leaders spend the majority of their time addressing the stated concerns and trying to justify the change. To effectively communicate and lead your team through change, it is necessary to address what's below the surface, to speak the unspoken, and to address both the surface and the subsurface fears head-on. There are several typical reactions to change, and the following models can be helpful for planning and framing your communications.

THE MARATHON EFFECT

Meg was on a board when a leadership crisis erupted. The board and CEO had hired an eventual replacement for the founder CEO, and the plan was for the outgoing and incoming CEOs to overlap for a year before the new leader officially assumed office. During that time, the incoming CEO discovered the founder CEO had not been truthful with the board on a variety of financial- and funding-related matters. When the issues emerged, the board chair decided to keep the matter close to the vest and only share it with the executive committee as opposed to the full board.

Approach change communication from a place of curiosity, empathy, and patience.

Over the next several months, the executive committee sought to work with the founder to exit peacefully and refrain from outing his unethical behavior. Ultimately, the committee's efforts proved futile when the founder CEO staged a dramatic "him versus me" stand-off in a board meeting and refused to budge. Meg was sure the rest of the board would side with the new leader because the founder's behavior was so egregious. In the end, they did not. They kept the founder and ousted the successor.

Meg ruminated on the experience for a long time. She came to understand the executive committee erred by not being transparent with the rest of the board as events unfolded. When the showdown occurred, the board had not traveled the same emotional distance as the executive committee. They had not been engaged in the struggle for several months. For many, it was their first time hearing about it, and they simply weren't ready to make such a huge decision. It turns out that what she experienced is called the Marathon Effect.

Through this lens, the executive committee was on mile marker 24. They had been running the race for months. But the rest of the board was still at the starting line.

This same scenario often plays out in companies when senior leaders spend months working toward a significant change initiative, only to have the announcement fall flat. We have observed this happen to numerous CEOs who are fatigued of thinking about an issue by the time they announce it, forget how much further along they are in their thought process, and, as a result, don't put enough energy and empathy into the communication. Executives get easily frustrated when employees do not quickly and eagerly adapt to changes. The reality is they need time to process the change. As the CEO, remember that your team has to travel the same distance you did to approve and adopt the change. This awareness will help you manage your communications accordingly and have a better outcome than Meg's board did.

THE SCARF MODEL

To frame change-related communications, we're big fans of David Rock's SCARF model,[24] which identifies five key areas where employees can feel threatened and have a fight-or-flight reaction. Your challenge (and opportunity) as a leader is to understand and address each of these key areas as they relate to the change you are trying to facilitate.

1. **Status**: Does this change impact my relative importance to others?

    Change can threaten employees' sense of status, making

them feel devalued or insecure. Approach change communication by recognizing and affirming the skills, contributions, and value of each team member. Highlighting how the change will provide opportunities for growth and development can help mitigate feelings of status loss.

2. **Certainty**: Does this change cause uncertainty?

Uncertainty is one of the most significant challenges in change management. You can address it by providing clear, consistent information about the change, why it's happening, and how it will unfold over time. Regular updates can help employees feel more secure about the future.

3. **Autonomy**: Does this change diminish my sense of independence and/or control over events?

People naturally resist when they feel controlled or powerless. To reduce or remove this threat, involve employees in the change process wherever possible. Offering choices, soliciting input, and allowing individuals or teams to have a say in how change is implemented enhances their sense of autonomy and engagement.

4. **Relatedness**: Does this change impact my psychological safety with others? (Are they friends or foes?)

Changes often disrupt hierarchies, relationships with authority, and social networks within an organization, leading to feelings of isolation or mistrust. One way to strengthen relationships is to create opportunities for team building, bonding, and collaboration. Emphasize shared goals and values and ensure everyone feels they are part of the journey.

5. Fairness: Does this change impact the perception of fairness? Will some be more impacted than others?

Having open communication about the rationale behind changes and creating opportunities to solicit and listen to employee concerns and suggestions can help maintain a sense of fairness.

When any of these five areas are impacted, an employee will start to close off and involuntarily be resistant to the change. By understanding these areas, you can structure your communication in a way that reduces the threat.

Based on the five stages of grief, the Kubler-Ross Change Curve captures the typical range of emotions employees go through when faced with significant change. It starts with shock and denial, then anger, bargaining, depression, and finally acceptance. Like the Marathon Effect, and the SCARF model, simply understanding that these are typical, normal, emotional reactions to change will help frame your approach to communicating. It's totally natural for employees to have initial resistance and experience uncertainty about a change. It doesn't mean the employees are not committed or they won't ultimately come around. They just need information and time to process the change and understand it.

BE RESPONSIVE, BUT NOT REACTIONARY

When employees are upset or make assumptions about change, it is common for CEOs to rush to placate concerns and quiet the gossip. Often, this results in off-the-cuff remarks or reactions in a Q&A session that later need to be walked back, which reduces credibility and employee trust in the process.

Employees need to have confidence the organization is led by someone with a clear vision and path forward. Constant pivots and retracted statements create doubt and uneasiness. It's okay if you don't have all the answers up front. Provide information early and often. Be thoughtful, intentional, and transparent about what you do know and actively move employees through the stages of change for the best results.

Amplifying Communication across the Four Stages of the Growth Gauntlet

Each stage of the Growth Gauntlet presents unique communication challenges. After all, it's much easier to ensure a message is delivered to and understood by a team of ten people than it is for a thousand people across multiple time zones. As a CEO, keep in mind the ever-evolving complexities of communication and adapt your communication strategy, style, and channels to what the company needs as it grows.

In the Emerge stage, communication generally flows directly from the founder to the team and back to the founder. Communication is frequent and informal, and information moves naturally and in real time as team members work closely with one another. Culture and knowledge transfer are a by-product of the team's cohesion.

Once the organization grows beyond the original small team and into the Operationalize stage, that informal, natural communication is no longer sufficient to reach all of the employees or to accomplish your strategy. The size of the team expands, departments become more formalized, and the number of layers on the org chart increases. Communication is still mostly top down, but leaders must become intentional about keeping everyone aligned and informed. Feedback from employees is solicited when there are problems. At this point, leaders discover whether employees are willing to share their thoughts, perceptions, and feedback openly and honestly.

Elevating their communication game is one of the biggest challenges CEOs face when transitioning from the Emerge to the Operationalize stage. One reason is that effective communication at this stage may require distancing yourself from people who are used to having full access to you, like some of those who helped you start the company.

When Meg first started at Google, founders Larry and Sergey were still accessible to the whole company. Anyone could email them or stop by their office, and they did. As the company grew, it became literally impossible for them to respond to every question, complaint, or idea from an employee. At this point in Google's growth, the founders had to systematize their communication for scale. What did this look like? Well, the first thing they did was hire an executive assistant to manage their calendars, emails, and meetings, and, perhaps most importantly, to serve as a bouncer for those would-be time assassins who stopped by the office wanting to hang out and chat like the old days. The volume of work Larry and Sergey faced running a larger and more complex organization forced them to clarify and differentiate their roles, each taking on separate responsibilities. They began to rely on a team of senior leaders to be a buffer and a conduit between them and the rest of the organization. And they started using more formal communications channels like regular Friday town hall meetings (called TGIF) in which they created a structured way to get in front of employees and talk about the company's strategy and performance, welcome "nooglers" (new hires), celebrate big wins, and field questions. Only by formalizing their communication were they able to elevate themselves as leaders and advance the organization.

In previous chapters, we've outlined specific communication systems that become important at the Operationalize stage such as onboarding practices, performance management, workflow processes, and so on. Each of these communication channels contributes to ensuring everyone has access to the information they need to do their jobs effectively, embrace the culture, and make the best decisions. CEOs must shift gears in the Operationalize stage to elevate their communications game by being intentional and strategic about it.

By the Thrive stage, the strategy shifts from an internal to an external focus, and the CEO often plays a significant role in communicating with the company's largest clients, vendors, and investors. These new target audiences require the CEO to build critical relationships and "sell" the company and strategy. Successful leaders are able to inspire confidence, display credible knowledge, and build authentic relationships with these outside constituencies to move the growth strategy forward. At this stage of growth, you'll begin to build out a communications team to help with messaging, writing remarks, and placing public relations pieces in the press. Internally, you'll want to continue regularly soliciting feedback from employees and using the information received to inform strategy and decisions. If employees are not openly providing negative feedback and ideas for improvement and innovation, enlist the help of an outside third party to do a cultural assessment.

By the time you reach the Explore and Expand stage, you're likely spending the majority of your time communicating to employees, customers, investors, the press, and so on. In fact, leaders who possess communication as a superpower are the most likely to make it all the way through the Growth Gauntlet. These are the leaders who understand the power of communication beyond just informing; they use it to educate, inspire, engage, and connect with a wide variety of stakeholders. We would argue that communication skills become more and more important as you progress through the Four Stages of Growth. They are what set great leaders apart from others.

Leveling Up: The Strategic Edge

Critical Questions for the CEO to Ask the Leadership Team

1. What do we need to communicate more clearly to employees?

2. Do we have processes in place to listen to employees?

3. What does our organization need to get smart on?

4. Are we intentional about using every touch point as an opportunity for reinforcing clarity and culture?

5. Do employees have the information they need to perform their jobs?

6. What communication systems might improve the flow of information in our organization?

7. In making organizational changes, have we factored in employees' reactions to the change using the SCARF model?

Critical Questions for the Board to Ask Regarding the CEO

1. Is the CEO an effective communicator? Do we feel informed, educated, engaged, and inspired by the communications we receive?

2. Is the CEO an inspirational leader? Are there areas of disconnect where the CEO and leadership team are further along on a change initiative than the rest of the organization?

3. Does the CEO inspire confidence from outside stakeholders?

Milestones and Initiatives

- Conduct regular town hall meetings.
- Develop employee recognition programs.
- Develop knowledge-sharing platforms (ERM, CRM, KMS).
- Brand internal communication and develop multiple channels.
- Conduct regular employee engagement surveys and listening sessions.

Amplify Communication Quick Reference

Stages of Growth			
Emerge Informal, Ad Hoc, Undefined, Reactive	**Operationalize** Defined, Data-Informed, Focused, Proactive	**Thrive** Accountable, Data-Driven, Predictable	**Explore & Expand** Strategic, Agile, Innovative, Opportunistic
Communication is informal, often direct from founder. Everyone is in-the-know because of the proximity of the small team. Customer communication is direct, tight loop.	Communication becomes more intentional though still largely top down. Employee and customer feedback are solicited episodically.	Communications protocols, channels, and systems emerge. Employee and customer feedback is regularly solicited and valued.	Comprehensive and strategic internal communications function exists for larger and more distributed customer base and workforce. Multi-directional feedback loops provide data that drives change.

What is it?

- Information Flow
- Knowledge Sharing
- Engagement
- Connection
- Inspiration
- Culture Transfer
- Change Management

What's the value?

Communication powers the Growth Gauntlet. It electrifies the grid. It's the currency or the energy that organizations run on. For CEOs, communication must be your superpower.

CHAPTER 8

Leveling Up:
The Strategic Edge

"The value of an idea lies in the using of it."

—Thomas Edison

IN THE LAST SEVERAL CHAPTERS, we have thoroughly explored the Six Imperatives for High Growth and how they evolve through the Four Stages of the Growth Gauntlet. It is our sincere hope the insights and ideas contained in the Growth Gauntlet framework have given you not only more clarity, but also greater confidence in navigating the inevitable challenges of high growth. We believe *the Growth Gauntlet IS the strategic edge* for successfully and sustainably taking your company to the next level.

In the pages that follow, we'll further share how you can use the Growth Gauntlet framework to put the insights and ideas we've shared in the previous chapters into action. Specifically, our intent is to guide leaders to do the following:

- Evaluate organizational maturity of a company to help make key decisions and determine priorities to allocate resources.

- Scale successfully and sustainably.

- Hire the right talent for the right stage of growth.

- Build strategic plans that take into consideration leveling up from one stage to the next.

- Align leadership around organizational development initiatives that create value.

The CEO's Edge

One way for you, as a CEO, to use the Growth Gauntlet is to determine where your company is on its growth journey, which informs what skills and achievements are needed to continue to grow, and whether there are any gaps between what is needed from the office of the CEO and your own personal passion and strengths. Successfully leading your team through the intense challenges of growth requires a strong vision, as well as internal clarity and alignment.

SELF-ALIGNMENT

Understanding the road ahead and taking a moment to candidly reflect on your own passion and strengths leads to insight about your company's path forward and the role to which you are best suited to position the company for growth. This self-reflection is particularly helpful as a company moves from the Emerge to Operationalize stage. The shift from an entrepreneurial focus to an operations and process focus can be a very challenging time.

In our experience, few CEOs are both incredible visionaries and detailed systems thinkers. If you don't know a shift is needed, you might continue to serve the company and pursue growth in the same ways you have in the past but find yourself struggling to achieve the same results. You work harder and harder, but without significant progress. For you, and every founder CEO, seeing the full scope and trajectory of the challenges heading your way in the Growth Gantlet is essential to determining how well your skills, strengths, and passions align with the company's needs. This knowledge allows you to choose the role you will play. You might decide to play the same role and hire someone with a different skill set to cover your blind spots. In many cases, CEOs have retained the innovator or business developer role and turned the systems and process building over to an experienced and proven operations executive.

There is no "right" way or universal path. Each way is entirely dependent on the unique needs of the organization, its current and future Stage of Growth, the strategy at hand, and the people in the roles. Using the Growth Gauntlet as a guide will help shed light on the best path for you and your business.

LEADERSHIP TEAM ALIGNMENT

The Growth Gauntlet is an especially effective framework for aligning the leadership team around a set of priorities and surfacing issues that need to be resolved. CEOs are only as strong as their leadership team, and the strength of that team depends on a variety of factors related to the Six Imperatives. The concepts we've explored thus far should have you ruminating, but you'll need the help and support of your leadership team to execute and level up.

"The Strategic Edge" questions we placed at the end of each chapter

> **CEOs are only as strong as their leadership team.**

emphasize the importance of CEOs knowing the strengths of their leadership teams and whether they are aligned with the organizational agenda. You've considered questions such as the following:

- Does my leadership team understand and are they aligned around the top three to five priorities of the business?
- If everyone continues to think and act the way they do, will we be able to achieve the results we want?
- Are we tolerating poor performers?

These questions provide a starting point for discussion. We suggest building a Growth Gauntlet retreat into your annual schedule to tackle these questions and give them the proper time, attention, and thorough consideration they require.

The Purpose of a Growth Gauntlet Retreat

- Gain alignment as a team on organizational strategy.
- Ensure everyone agrees on where the company is on the Growth Gauntlet.
- Plan for navigating the current Stage of the Growth Gauntlet.
- Prepare for moving to the next stage.
- Move forward with value-creating priorities.

Ahead of the leadership retreat, it's useful to poll the team using a short survey based on the Six Imperatives. Often, the leadership team does not agree on everything, and these gaps are a good place to dig in and spend some time. For example, if you find team members are rating the maturity of the Six Imperatives differently, it suggests some parts of the organization are more mature than others. A majority of team members might feel the organization is in the Thrive stage for Elevate Talent, but one leader feels her department is still in the Operationalize stage. Perhaps her department has been slower to adopt talent management practices than others. The Growth Gauntlet brings this type of discrepancy to light. With this knowledge, the leader can prioritize talent management and the team can hold her accountable for catching up with the others.

We saw a similar level of enlightenment occur when the leadership team of a data center company took the short Growth Gauntlet survey in preparation for their retreat. Asked about goal setting, six out of seven of them chose "We have no formal goal setting." Interestingly, as they dug into the issue, they discovered the CEO was the outlier. He believed there was a formal goal-setting process because he set the goals every year. His team, on the other hand, did not believe there was a process, because, as it was revealed, they weren't involved in it. The CEO consulted each member of his leadership team individually before setting the goals, but the group had a strong desire to set the strategy and goals collaboratively. This marked a milestone in the company's growth when the CEO chose to involve the whole team in setting goals and objectives—a key milestone in moving toward true, distributed leadership (as discussed in Chapter 4).

Insights like the one mentioned previously are important, but without action, they're just notes on a whiteboard.

You'll want to carve out time during the retreat to help the team do the following:

- Reflect on the insights they've surfaced.

- Determine what's most important to pursue.

- Create specific action steps to hold the team accountable.

Memorializing the agreed-upon objectives, key results, and accountabilities allows the team to convert ideas into action.

STRATEGIC PLANNING

The Growth Gauntlet is also a valuable guide for strategic planning. The framework provides the infrastructure blueprint for your people strategy. It incorporates the evolution of an organization's focus (vision and strategic business goals) and structure (organizational, composition of leadership team, and processes), and it identifies the talent and culture needed to grow successfully.

Our friend Matt Crow, CEO of a valuation company, was preparing to take his team through a strategic-planning process when he came across the Growth Gauntlet. In reviewing it, Matt found his firm's history closely mirrored the Stages of the Growth Gauntlet presented in the framework, and it helped him understand when they were about to enter a new stage. He used the Growth Gauntlet to frame the conversation with his team and guide their preparations for the challenges ahead. Looking toward a move into the Explore and Expand stage over the next several years, Matt's team was able to reflect on each of the Six Imperatives and think about how to level up the organization. These conversations led to specific and tangible goals for the strategic plan, including adding their first HR professional to the team, which meant they were prepared for the challenges of the Growth Gauntlet.

When it's time to create your next strategic plan, the Growth Gauntlet is a comprehensive guide for setting the direction of your company. Ultimately, if you are the CEO of a high-growth, private equity-backed company, your goal is to create value. Jim Tallman, a former CEO and a current board chair of a SaaS company, said this to us on the matter: "If you're in the venture capital phase, or you're in the growth equity phase, there is one thing and one thing only in the private equity world: value creation. It is the only objective."

The key to creating value is developing and leveraging the full potential of your people. People drive results. Tallman also said, "Value creation is about the value you create with your customer and your employees."

If we were discussing value creation with a residential builder, he would talk about building beautiful bathrooms and kitchens, which sell houses every time. In private equity, investors want a strong leadership team, a strong business model, a sustainable organization, and double-digit growth. Investors are generally finance people who are adept at assessing a company's financials and looking at comparable companies to determine value. But they lack the same calculus to apply to the human side of the equation. The Growth Gauntlet provides that measure. The more mature the company is in its organizational development, the greater its value.

The Board's Edge

Taking on investment capital provides founders with more than just funding. It often brings a formalized board made up of experienced investors and independent directors. Investors also introduce, as discussed, an increased focus on value creation for shareholders.

The board is responsible for overseeing the strategy and direction of the company and monitoring whether the company is meeting its objectives. Management reports regularly to the board on metrics and milestones related to these areas. For a company to grow successfully, the board and the CEO must establish a trusting relationship and align around the strategic growth plan for the business. When the board and CEO have a strong, trusting relationship, they can weather the challenges that inevitably come with growth.

The Growth Gauntlet framework is useful for facilitating candid conversations between the board and CEO about the state of the company and what is needed to create value. As veteran board chair Jim Bradley told us, "The Growth Gauntlet provides a systematic way to think about where you are and where you're going, just like a scoreboard." Regarding the relationship with CEOs, Bradley said, "When I'm dealing with founder CEOs, I often have to say, 'You've done an awesome job, but you cannot be in on every sale if we're going to get to $50 million.' These CEOs are the visionaries, the product people, and it's one of the things that make them so successful early on. But the reality is, 'I need 25 salespeople to do what you do if we're going to get to $100 million.'"

The Growth Gauntlet also helps to objectively clarify what skills are needed to create the value and infrastructure to grow the business to the next stage. Jim Bradley tells us, "I'm often dealing with a situation where I'm trying to tell the CEO it can't work the way it has been. And I'm getting more than average resistance. But we're starting to hit a plateau on value creation that could make this a longer-term waste of time. The Growth Gauntlet helps a board and the CEO understand that different skill sets are required at different stages in a company's growth trajectory." Like the soccer coach we referenced in Chapter 4, the Growth Gauntlet helps to normalize the fact that boards often bring in leaders with different skill sets at key inflection points as the company enters a new stage.

As a CEO, you wear three primary hats: your personal hat, your CEO hat, and your shareholder hat. Sometimes these roles are at odds with one another. Sometimes these hats fit differently. There are times when what the business needs is not in sync with where you're most effective personally. As an experienced private equity investor and board member told us, "Sometimes I have to point out to a founder CEO it's in his best interest as a shareholder to pass his CEO hat to a more experienced executive to grow the business."

Investors' Edge: Due Diligence

Many investors tout the high value they place on leadership and teams, but most due diligence processes focus on digging into the target company's products, finances, and technologies. The Growth Gauntlet provides a structured and holistic lens through which to evaluate the company's human capital. Insights from this process help investors to develop a comprehensive plan to drive growth, maximize return on investment in the future, and potentially avoid costly errors.

During the due diligence phase, investors use the Growth Gauntlet as a guide for conducting in-depth discovery on the following:

- What stage of the Growth Gauntlet is the company in (or between)?

- What organizational infrastructure (framed by the Six Imperatives) already exists and what is needed? Can we identify and prioritize short-term and long-term challenges and opportunities?

- What is each leader's role and what hats do they wear?
  What is each person's highest and best purpose (professionally and personally) so we can make sure we have the right talent in the right roles optimized for growth?

The responses to this targeted line of inquiry provide three layers of insight. First, you are able to home in on where the organization is in its growth journey and establish a baseline from which to plan and grow. From there, we get an understanding of where the leadership team is aligned and where they are not. For example, did everyone agree the company was in the Emerge stage when discussing Elevating Talent, or was there disagreement? What can we learn from areas or topics where the executives disagree? Are some areas of the company more developed than others? What is the leadership team's ability to grow and execute the strategy?

Second, by diving into the Six Imperatives, you will gain clarity as to whether the executives see the path forward or are unsure of the next step. Do their skills align with what needs to be accomplished? Likely, there is significant organizational infrastructure to be built out such as adding a sales and support team, becoming a self-replicating talent machine, or simply producing a predictable financial forecast. Does the leadership team have the skills and experience necessary to make the appropriate hires and shepherd those initiatives? Using the Six Imperatives has the added advantage of introducing a common language for the duration of the investor/executive partnership. It helps to set expectations and get everyone aligned around the Stage of Growth the company is in and the priorities necessary for scaling.

The third insight gained through Growth Gauntlet due diligence is around leadership team structure and function. As discussed, early-stage growth companies are full of people who wear many hats. Understanding who has what skills and experiences is critical to staffing for growth. You might find, for example, a key leader is managing multiple functions including Finance and HR, but has no real expertise or desire to do HR. Such insight will inform what you do with the HR function going forward. Knowing who is on the executive team, where they thrive, and what they're interested in pursuing is critical information in the due diligence stage. It helps investors understand what it will take to build the business and hit the ground running quickly, post-close.

In a recent example, investors used the Growth Gauntlet to determine they needed a CEO with a different skill set than the skill set possessed by the sitting CEO, though they recognized he was incredibly valuable to the business. Using the Growth Gauntlet to frame the conversation, the investors helped the CEO understand the role was evolving away from his skill set and toward one more centered on financial reporting, driving revenue, and reporting to the board. He knew the job was not one he was prepared for or would enjoy. Though initially the wind went out of his sails, he understood the rationale for the change. Once the company's focus and strategy were clear, the investors and CEO were free to discuss alternative roles. They settled upon a product role that energized him and utilized his talents. In short, he found his highest and best purpose.

In another example, a COO was managing sales, operations, finance, accounting, HR, and customer success, basically, everything but product and technology. In our experience, very few people with this varied set of responsibilities are either good at all of them or enjoy them all, which was absolutely true for this COO. When asked which hats she'd most like to discard, she did not hesitate: HR,

A/P, and A/R. When asked where she derived the most energy, she said sales strategy and account management. Armed with this new information, the investors decided to hire an HR coordinator and a controller so the COO could focus on building out a sales team and driving revenue.

The Growth Gauntlet framework also helps investors learn which employees the executives consider to be key people within the organization. We often ask, "Who can't you live without?" This information allows us to make a list of key employees who might need some extra incentives in the form of equity grants or stay bonuses to stick with the company through the transitions. These are also the first people to meet with once the deal closes, to let them know how valued they are, and to get their insights.

RISK MITIGATION

Using the Growth Gauntlet during due diligence also helps with risk mitigation. The Six Imperatives provide a different angle from which to ask questions and dig into matters related to focus, culture, leadership, talent, structure, and communication. You'll be surprised by what you might uncover.

We once discovered a CEO was promoted to his position through a backroom wager with the founder. His lack of experience was a material risk to the business. More often, you'll find out who has the trust and confidence of the team, who plans on leaving as soon as the deal is signed, and who is jockeying for a promotion. These kinds of issues are important for investors to address ahead of a transaction if they're fortunate enough to find out about them.

POST-CLOSE DEEP DIVE

Once the deal is signed, the work turns toward validating assumptions made in the limited scope of the pre-close diligence process and putting together a growth plan to scale the organization. One of the biggest challenges investors face is they do not have access to the entire employee base ahead of making the decision to buy the company. And to complicate matters, before a transaction is signed, companies and investors are still in the "courting phase" and often reluctant to disclose anything that might sour the deal. Once the deal is signed, investors are committed. With full access to the wider employee base, it's important to take the time to do a deep dive using the Growth Gauntlet as a guide.

Post-close due diligence is similar to pre-close due diligence but with a wider scope. Instead of zeroing in on the leadership team, the focus shifts post-close to the entire employee population. Whether through individual conversations, focus groups, or surveys, it's important to connect with and discover the insights, perceptions, and observations of every employee in the company. From an investor's position, the most obvious benefit of including everyone in the process is to collect as much information as possible to learn more about the state of the company and what is needed to grow.

Another additional and important benefit of this work is the trust and goodwill investors can build by listening to the employees. The truth is that a change in ownership creates deep-rooted levels of uncertainty. Don't assume that employees of the acquired company will automatically accept new leadership or "opt in" to a new plan. New owners—no matter how hands-off they intend to be—need to put forth the effort to listen and learn.

Surveying the wider employee base serves the same purpose as it does with the leadership team: information gathering, building trust through listening, and valuing employees' experience and opinions. Surveys can take many forms. Whichever form you decide upon, we recommend the survey encompasses the following five steps:

1. Collaborate with leadership to develop the survey.

2. Communicate with employees about the survey and its importance.

3. Analyze survey results and distill the data into broad insights.

4. Prioritize issues based on urgency, impact, time, and resources.

5. Communicate the survey results and plans for change to all employees.

As we said earlier, the last step is particularly important and often overlooked. If you ask for the employees' thoughts, it's important to come back to the group to effectively say, "This is what you said, and this is what we're going to do about it." You will squander all of your trust and goodwill if people's voices, observations, and experiences do not translate into action.

Investors who take the time at the outset of the investment to look carefully under the hood and thoroughly assess what they have bought will be able to build trust, proactively close gaps, and pre-emptively solve problems, which makes for a much smoother ride in the first year of growth.

Yes, leading (and/or investing in) a high-growth business can feel like running a gauntlet. We know. We've been there; we've helped others who have been there, and we're always on the lookout for new and emerging challenges as market dynamics, industry break-throughs, and global economic variables continue to shift and evolve.

Through our work with a wide variety of highly capable and entrepreneurial CEOs, investors, and board members across multiple sectors, we've discovered the Growth Gauntlet framework and its Six Imperatives for high growth offer executives *the strategic edge* necessary to survive the never-ending challenges of growth, gain and maintain a competitive advantage, grow sustainably and profitably, and attract investment capital. By digging into the concepts and implementing the strategies presented here, we're confident you'll have the tools and the knowledge necessary to create long-term value and thrive in the face of whatever obstacles and opportunities are thrown your way.

Running the Gauntlet

"A management style that works brilliantly at a ten-person company can destroy a thousand-person company."

—Morgan Housel, *Same as Ever*

OVER THE COURSE of this book, we have introduced you to the Six Imperatives and charted their evolution across the Four Stages of the Growth Gauntlet. More than anything, we hope you will take away that people drive results and context is *everything*. Whether you are a CEO, an investor, or a board member, looking at an organization through the lens of the Growth Gauntlet will help you understand where you are on your growth journey, and that knowledge will provide valuable context for every strategic decision you make—from hiring to strategic planning to investment.

In his 2023 book, *Same as Ever: A Guide to What Never Changes,* Morgan Housel writes, "A management style that works brilliantly at a ten-person company can destroy a thousand-person company, which is a hard lesson to learn when some companies grow that fast in a few short years. Travis Kalanick, the former CEO of Uber, is a great example. No one but him was capable of growing the company early on, and anyone but him was needed as the company matured." This is the great paradox of growth, which takes us back to the Marshall Goldsmith truism we placed at the very beginning of this book: "What got you here won't get you there."[25] We hope the Growth Gauntlet demystifies what *will* get you there.

At its core, the Growth Gauntlet is a people-focused organizational maturity model. As Housel referenced, organizations mature just like people do, and there's a reason we don't give toddlers a driver's license. An organization must develop and then strengthen certain organizational competencies for it to scale successfully. Developing and reinforcing a sustainable culture, becoming a self-replicating talent machine, establishing processes that yield consistent predictable results, and creating outlets for people to provide valuable feedback are just some of the core competencies a stable and scalable organization demonstrates. These (and other) critical competencies are built systematically, one step at a time, by leaders who are clear about their mission and self-aware about what is needed for the role they play.

Most entrepreneurs come to leadership from disciplines other than people management. Successful entrepreneurs who remain with the company as it grows and evolves are active students of people management. They recognize the path to elevating the company is paved through their ability to mobilize, motivate, and move people to action. The Six Imperatives offer strategic levers for thoughtful leaders to effect growth and manage change. We encourage you to share and socialize the Growth Gauntlet within your leadership teams so they may adopt a common language around organizational maturity. Once the Growth Gauntlet becomes ingrained in your organizational lexicon, you'll start to see your obstacles and opportunities through its context.

Virtually every conversation we have with high-growth CEOs leads us back to the Gauntlet framework. Just recently, Meg was interviewing a candidate for a CFO role. Her resume indicated she had mostly worked for mature organizations in the Growth or Expand stages. The company she was interviewing to work for was trying to make it through the Operationalize stage, and the finance function, in particular, was a mess. The Growth Gauntlet framework helped to shape the cadence and content of the interview. Specifically, why would she want to work for a company in the Operationalize stage? Did she know what she was getting into? Did she understand she wouldn't have a large support team to rely on? She'd have to roll up her sleeves and perform tasks she probably hadn't performed in years. On paper, and relative to the other candidates, she was the highest performer with the most experience. Many teams would have made her an offer on the spot and be grateful someone of her caliber was even interested. But understanding the context of what the company needed in the CFO role for the Operationalize stage is critical to making the right selection. Hiring someone whose ambitions, experience, and expectations don't align with the actual requirements of the role is a waste of everyone's time and resources.

The Growth Gauntlet is a map to guide your work through the milestones and initiatives, in a pace and a manner consistent with your culture and vision. Ultimately, we want you to be successful, your employees to be content, and your business to grow. Our greatest hope is the Growth Gauntlet spares you the time, cost, and anxiety of wondering what's next, and assures you're not alone. Growth is hard. We hope this book will make it just a little easier.

Acknowledgments

THIS BOOK IS THE SUM of our collective experiences. We would not be here without the career opportunities we have enjoyed—for Howard, pursuing a career in the law and working with the exceptional attorneys and clients of Glankler Brown and Kiesewetter Wise; and for Meg, learning from and working with the diverse and brilliant colleagues at Credit Suisse First Boston, Applied Semantics, and Google. Each of these opportunities has been a vital part of our story, and we are indebted to the successes (and failures!) that taught us so much.

We are grateful for our many clients over the years whose stories, successes, and challenges helped us develop the Growth Gauntlet framework.

We are especially grateful to Casey West, Hunter Witherington, Ed Nenon, Chris McGanity, and the team at SSM Partners for their commitment, as investors, to building great teams, and their belief that people drive value creation. Their interest in and enthusiasm for our work helped us to realize the value of the Growth Gauntlet framework and, ultimately, to write this book. A special shoutout to Jordan Purdham for quarterbacking our survey of over 1,000 companies and crunching the results.

We appreciate our advisors, mentors, and colleagues who are executives, investors, and board members and who lent their wisdom and experiences to this book. Thanks to Jim Lackey, Jim Bradley, Jim Tallman, Darren Schulte, Michael Burkhold, Carl Hoburg, Chris Connell, Derek Smith, Leigh Silver, Tom Wicka, Eric Harber, Christopher Redhage, Mike Madden, Alan Morse, Robert Covington, Matt Crow, Sam Graham, Chris Crosby, Bo White, Dr. Micky Quinones, Dr. Bob Waller, Patrick Hamner, Jeanne Gray Carr, John Daniel, Barham Ray, Wilson Orr, Mike Bruns, Bena Cates, Milton Lovell, Michael Graber, Mark Levine, Molly Crosby, Ben Pirmann, John Wittber, and Bob Moore.

Our heartfelt thanks to the one and only Beth Brock, our business manager and chief cheerleader, whose tireless efforts wrangling us made all the difference. We literally could not have done this without her.

We owe a debt of gratitude to our former partners and PeopleCap alumni who helped advance our thinking: Coleman Barton, Anna McQuiston, Andy Nix, and Katie Spencer. We are better because we worked with you and learned from you.

Most especially we want to thank our kitchen cabinet, trusted advisors Matt Crow, Sam Graham, Casey West, Hunter Witherington, and Dr. John Whittemore, who took the time to read an early draft and give us meaningful feedback that shaped future drafts. Your wisdom and encouragement gave us confidence. This book (and its title!) is better because of you!

Our book journey was circuitous and serendipitous. We met Alicia Dunams at a conference several years ago when all we had were aspirations of writing a book. When we found our topic, we reconnected with her and participated in her workshop, "Bestseller in a Weekend," which helped us get those first words on the page.

Later, when we were a bit stuck, our friend, author and coach Jon Chandonnet, gave us some advice—find a developmental editor. We did find one! Our fabulous developmental editor and project MVP Brooke White put us firmly on the path to success. She expertly guided us through completing the manuscript and helped us navigate the publishing process. From there, the excellent team at Greenleaf ushered us across the finish line. Truly, this book is the result of a great team effort.

We have immeasurable gratitude to our beloved families for their patience with us as we squirreled away to write and their encouragement to get it done. To our spouses, Scott and Cindy, thank you for believing in us and supporting our work. You are the foundation that makes everything possible. Thank you to our parents, Pam & Howard Cleveland, Nancy & Jimmy Thomas, and Margaret & Fred Ridolphi, for instilling in us unlimited curiosity and a strong desire to help others. We are grateful for our original confidantes and advisors, our sisters, Scott Thomas Montgomery and Amy Cleveland Shoaf. To our kids, Alex, Elizabeth, Andrew, Lucy, and Tom, we hope this book will prove useful to each of you in your careers one day. Never stop learning!

Meg's mother, Margaret, was often quoted as saying about any challenging endeavor, "It will be a nice thing to *have done*." This book certainly fits that description—we are grateful to have done it!

Bibliography

Anthony, Scott D., Clark G. Gilbert, and Mark W. Johnson. *Dual Transformation: How to Reposition Today's Business While Creating the Future*. Boston, Massachusetts: Harvard Business Review Press, 2017.

Bock, Laszlo. *Work Rules! Insights from Inside Google That Will Transform How You Live and Lead*. New York: Hachette Book Group, 2015.

Burton, Richard M., Borge Obel, and Gerardine DeSanctis. *Organizational Design: A Step-by-Step Approach*. 2nd ed. New York: Cambridge University Press, 2011.

Chandler, Alfred D. *Strategy & Structure: Chapters in the History of American Industrial Enterprise*. Washington, DC: Beard Books, 1962.

Cloud, Henry. *Boundaries: When to Say Yes How to Say No to Take Control of Your Life*. Grand Rapids, MI: Zondervan, 2017.

Collins, Jim. *Good to Great: Why Some Companies Make the Leap . . . and Others Don't*. New York: Harper Collins Publishers, 2001.

Collins, Jim and Jerry Porras. "Building Your Company's Vision." *Harvard Business Review*, September–October 1996, pp. 65–77.

Doerr, John. *Measure What Matters*. New York: Portfolio Penguin, 2018.

Drucker, Peter. *The Five Most Important Questions You Will Ever Ask about Your Organization*. San Francisco, California: Jossey-Bass, 2008.

Gerstner, Louis V. *Who Says Elephants Can't Dance?* New York: HarperCollins, 2003.

Goldsmith, Marshall. *What Got You Here Won't Get You There*. New York: Hachette Books, 2007.

Gruenert, Steve and Todd Whitaker. *School Culture Rewired*. Alexandria, Virginia: ASCD, 2015.

Hoffman, Reid and Chris Yeh. *Blitzscaling: The Lightning-Fast Path to Building Massively Valuable Companies*. New York: Penguin Random House, 2018.

Housel, Morgan. *Same as Ever: A Guide to What Never Changes*. New York: Penguin Random House, 2023.

Jacob, Kathryn, Sue Unerman, and Mark Edwards. *Belonging: The Key to Transforming and Maintaining Diversity, Inclusion and Equality at Work*. London, United Kingdom: Bloomsbury Publishing, 2020.

Kübler-Ross, Elisabeth. *On Death and Dying: What the Dying Have to Teach Doctors, Nurses, Clergy, and Their Own Family*. New York: Scribner, 1969.

Lencioni, Patrick. *The Five Dysfunctions of a Team: A Leadership Fable*. San Francisco, California: Jossey-Bass, 2002.

Lencioni, Patrick. *Death by Meeting: A Leadership Fable*. San Francisco, California: Jossey-Bass, 2004.

Rock, David and Al H. Ringleb. *Handbook of NeuroLeadership*. New York: Dr. David Rock and Dr. Al H. Ringleb, 2013.

Schein, Edgar. *The Corporate Culture Survival Guide*. San Francisco, California: Jossey-Bass, 1999.

Schein, Edgar. *Organizational Culture and Leadership*. San Francisco, California: Jossey-Bass, 2010.

Schmidt, Eric and Jonathan Rosenberg. *How Google Works*. New York: Hachette Book Group, 2014.

Scott, Kim. *Radical Candor: Be a Kick-Ass Boss without Losing Your Humanity*. New York: St Martin's Press, 2017.

Smart, Geoff and Randy Street. *Who: The A Method for Hiring*. New York: Ballantine Books, 2008.

Weinfurter, D. J. "The Keys to Effective Leadership," in *Second Stage Entrepreneurship*. New York: Palgrave Macmillan, 2013. https://doi.org/10.1007/978-1-137-33714-6_12.

Wickman, Gino. *Traction: Get a Grip on Your Business*. Dallas, Texas: BenBella Books, 2011.

Other Sources

Schein, Edgar. "Quote Organizational Culture and Leadership." 1985. https://en.wikiquote.org/wiki/Edgar_H._Schein, p. 11.

Sinek, Simon. LinkedIn Post. https://www.linkedin.com/posts/simonsinek_before-we-can-build-the-world-we-want-to-activity-6763462934313111552-Awdj?utm_source=share&utm_medium=member_desktop.

Endnotes

1. Reid Hoffman and Chris Yeh, *Blitzscaling: The Lightning-Fast Path to Building Massively Valuable Companies* (Penguin Random House, 2018).

2. Google, "About Google," https://about.google/; Nike, "What Is Nike's Mission?" https://www.nike.com/help/a/nikeinc-mission; Amazon, "Who We Are," https://www.aboutamazon.com /about-us; Business Strategy Hub, "Apple Mission Statement | Vision | Core Values | Strategy (2024 Analysis)," https:// bstrategyhub.com/apple-mission-statement-vision-core-values/.

3. Jim Collins and Jerry Porras, "Building Your Company's Vision," *Harvard Business Review*, September–October 1996.

4. "Business Level and Corporate Level Strategies of Google Marketing Essay," UKEssays.com, January 1, 2015, https:// us.ukessays.com/essays/marketing/business-level-and -corporate-level-strategies-of-google-marketing-essay. php#:~:text=Google's%20Corporate%20Strategy%20is%20 to,called%20as%20corporate%20strategic%20planning.

5. Shawn Cox, "Nike Ups Its Game: Understanding the Keys to Nike's Sustained Success," McMillan Doolittle, August 3, 2023, https://www.mcmillandoolittle.com/nike-ups-its-game -understanding-the-keys-to-nikes-sustained-success/.

6. Riya, "Understanding Amazon Business Strategy," Feedough, August 7, 2023, https://www.feedough.com/understanding -amazon-business-strategy/.

7. Daniel Pereira, "Apple Mission and Vision Statement," The Business Model Analyst, August 27, 2024, https:// businessmodelanalyst.com/apple-mission-and-vision-statement/.

8. Edgar Schein, *Organizational Culture and Leadership* (Jossey-Bass, 2010).

9. David Cummings, "The Top 3 Things Every Entrepreneur Needs to Know," *David Cummings on Startups* (blog), December 7, 2011, https://davidcummings.org/2011/12/07/the-top-3 -things-every-entrepreneur-needs-to-know/.

10. Louis V. Gerstner, *Who Says Elephants Can't Dance?* (HarperCollins, 2003).

11. Ben Horowitz, "Your Mission Statement Is Not Your Company Culture," *Medium*, October 30, 2019, https://marker.medium .com/your-mission-statement-is-not-your-company-culture -c5980c1b530c.

12. Heather Somerville and Joseph Menn, "Uber CEO Travis Kalanick Resigns under Investor Pressure," Reuters, June 21, 2017, https:// www.reuters.com/article/technology/uber-ceo -travis-kalanick-resigns-under-investor-pressure -idUSKBN19C0G6/.

13. "Disney's Four Keys to a Great Guest Experience," World Class Benchmarking, https://worldclassbenchmarking.com/disneys -four-keys-to-a-great-guest-experience/.

14. Alok Patel and Stephanie Plowman, "The Increasing Importance of a Best Friend at Work," Gallup, August 17, 2022, https://www. gallup.com/workplace/397058/increasing-importance -best-friend-work.aspx%20WORKPLACE.

15. Eric Schmidt and Jonathan Rosenberg, *How Google Works* (Hachette Book Group, 2014).

16. "ASLA 2006 Student Awards," American Society of Landscape Architects, https://www.asla.org/awards/2006/studentawards /282.html.

17. Richard M. Burton, Børge Obel, and Gerardine DeSanctis, *Organizational Design: A Step-by-Step Approach*, 2nd ed. (Cambridge University Press, 2011).

18. Rick Tetzeli, "Mary Barra Is Remaking GM's Culture and the Company Itself," *Fast Company*, October 17, 2016, https://www .fastcompany.com/3064064/mary-barra-is-remaking-gms -culture-and-the-company-itself.

19. Charles Osgood, "Responsibility Poem van Charles Osgood," Organization Builders, https://www.organizationbuilders.com /content1/responsibiltypoem.

20. Robert Sher, "Never Leave Internal Communications to Chance in Midsized Companies," *Forbes*, July 17, 2014, https://www .forbes.com/sites/robertsher/2014/07/17/never-leave-internal -communications-to-chance-in-midsized-companies/#:~:text= A%20Towers%20Watson%20study%20(Capitalizing,the%20 firms%20that%20are%20least.

21. Alok Patel and Stephanie Plowman, "The Increasing Importance of a Best Friend at Work," Gallup, August 17, 2022, https://www. gallup.com/workplace/397058/increasing-importance -best-friend-work.aspx%20WORKPLACE.

22. Madison Williams, "Erin Andrews Explains Why She's 'Obsessed' with Brian Daboll," *Sports Illustrated*, January 2, 2023, https://www.si.com/extra-mustard/2023/01/02/erin-andrews -explains-obsessed-brian-daboll-new-york-giants.

23. David Leonard and Claude Coltea, "Most Change Initiatives Fail—but They Don't Have To," Gallup, May 24, 2013, https:// news.gallup.com/businessjournal/162707/change-initiatives-fail- don.aspx.

24. David Rock, *Your Brain at Work* (HarperCollins, 2009).

25. Marshall Goldsmith, *What Got You Here Won't Get You There* (Hachette Books, 2007).

About the Authors

Howard Cleveland
Principal and Co-Founder
howard.cleveland@peoplecap.com

Howard is a seasoned strategist who serves as a coach and trusted advisor to leaders navigating complex transitions and facing high-stakes decisions. Drawing on his unique blend of experience in employment law, executive coaching, and people strategy, Howard helps leaders identify the underlying dynamics and strategic opportunities in their challenges, empowering them to lead more effectively.

Meg Thomas Crosby
Principal and Co-Founder
meg.crosby@peoplecap.com

Meg is a recognized thought leader in people strategy. She is a strategic advisor to CEOs, boards, and investors, and enjoys asking tough questions. She sits on multiple corporate and nonprofit boards and serves as an Operating Partner with SSM Partners, a growth equity firm focused on investing in software, services, and healthcare companies. During her 20-year career in human resources, she has worked for companies of all shapes and sizes, including a global Wall Street investment bank, a small tech start-up in Los Angeles, and Google.